Immigration Made Simple

Immigration Made Simple

an easy to read guide to the U.S. Immigration process

fourth edition

by Barbara Brooks Kimmel and Alan M. Lubiner, Esq.

Published by:
Next Decade, Inc.
39 Old Farmstead Road
Chester, New Jersey 07930-2732 USA

Cover design by Lily Secada, Secada Creative, Greenwich, Connecticut

Publisher's Cataloging in Publication
(prepared by Quality Books Inc.)

Kimmel, Barbara Brooks
  Immigration made simple: an easy to read guide to the U.S.
immigration process/ by Barbara Brooks Kimmel & Alan M.
Lubiner-- 4th ed.
 p. cm.
Includes index.
Preassigned LCCN: 97-75380
ISBN 0-9626003-4-2

  1. Emigration and immigration law-- United States-- Popular
works.   I. Lubiner, Alan M. II. Title

KF4819.6.K56 1998   342. 73'082
                                        QBI97-41444

$19.95 Softcover

Table of Contents

About The Authors

• Barbara Kimmel spent fifteen years employed in the New York area, as an immigration consultant, with many international companies and several prominent immigration lawyers. During that time she successfully guided thousands of aliens through the immigration process. In 1990 Barbara began writing, publishing and distributing books on immigration, citizenship and related subjects. This is the fourth edition of **Immigration Made Simple,** first published in 1990. Her book has received outstanding professional reviews, and has been a Quality Books #1 bestseller. Barbara is also the co-author of **Citizenship Made Simple**, published in 1996. Finally, she is the President and Publisher at Next Decade, Inc. in Chester, New Jersey. Her company was named **Publisher of the Year** at the 1997 Book Expo in Chicago.

Ms. Kimmel holds a Bachelor of Arts Degree in International Affairs from Lafayette College in Pennsylvania and a Master's Degree in Business Administration from the Bernard M. Baruch Graduate School of Business of the City University of New York.

• Alan Lubiner has been practicing Immigration Law since 1975. From 1975 until 1981, he was employed by the Immigration & Naturalization Service in a number of capacities including assisting in the drafting of legislation for the Select Commission on Immigration in Washington, DC. He also spent time in the United States Attorney's Office in the Southern District of Florida where he served as a Special Assistant United States Attorney assigned to special Immigration prosecutions.

In 1981, Mr. Lubiner opened a private law practice, specializing in Immigration law. His main office is located in Kenilworth, New Jersey. Mr. Lubiner's practice is heavily concentrated in professionals. He currently represents major corporations, individuals and universities in the scientific field with emphasis on computer science, electrical engineering, chemical engineering, chemistry and pharmaceutical research. He has successfully handled over 1000 cases for foreign students and other individuals.

Mr. Lubiner holds a Bachelor of Science Degree in Finance from New York University and a Juris Doctorate degree from Brooklyn Law School. He is a member of the American Immigration Lawyers Association, an affiliated organization of the American Bar Association, and served on its Board of Governors. He is a past Chairman of the New Jersey Chapter of the American Immigration Lawyer's Association. Mr. Lubiner is a member of the Bar of the States of New Jersey, New York and Pennsylvania and is admitted to practice before the Federal Courts in New Jersey, New York and Pennsylvania, as well as the United States Supreme Court. Finally, he is the co-author of **Immigration Made Simple** and **Citizenship Made Simple.**

*With special thanks to all those who continue to recognize
the importance of this valuable reference book*

****

Disclaimer

The purpose of this book is to provide interested individuals with a basic understanding of the rules and regulations concerning U.S. Immigration procedures. It is sold with the understanding that the publisher and authors are not engaged in rendering legal or other professional services in this book, only in sharing information in regard to the subject matter covered. If legal or other expert assistance is required, the services of a competent professional should be sought.

This manual was not written to provide all the information that is available to the authors/and or publisher, but to compliment, amplify and supplement other texts and available information. While every effort has been made to ensure that this book is as complete and accurate as possible, there may be mistakes, either typographical or in content. Therefore, this text should be used as a general guide only, and not as the ultimate source of U.S. Immigration information. Furthermore, this book contains information on U.S. Immigration only up to the printing date. The rules and regulations change frequently.

The authors and Next Decade, Inc. shall not be held liable, nor be responsible to any person or entity with respect to any loss or damage caused, or alleged to be caused, directly or indirectly by the information contained in this book.

If you do not wish to be bound by the above, you may return this book to the publisher for a full refund.

Preface

Over the past fifteen years I have helped hundreds of people from every corner of the world process petitions for temporary and permanent U.S. visas. These individuals included students, trainees, and entry level employees. Others were sophisticated investors and senior executives.

Interestingly, all of the people mentioned above, regardless of their backgrounds, shared one common characteristic. They lacked the necessary knowledge of the U.S. Immigration process. Because of this, one question has continuously been asked of me. Isn't there a reference book that I can read and use as a guide in the future, a simple manual that will provide me with a basic understanding of immigration? I could not give them a recommendation that really met those needs, and so in 1990 I published the first edition of **Immigration Made Simple**. I received thousands of orders from every state in the U.S., and many foreign countries as well...and now I can recommend a book that finally meets this need!

At the end of 1990, President George Bush signed a bill, called the "Immigration Act of 1990", which represented the most sweeping change in U.S. Immigration regulations in over fifty years. The number of people who became entitled to immigrate to the U.S. increased by more than 30%. **Immigration Made Simple** (1992 edition) was rewritten to include many of the new and interim INS regulations. Over the next four years, many administrative changes took place in the processing of immigration applications, and this lead to the publication of the third edition of **Immigration Made Simple** in 1996. Over the past two years additional administrative changes have been enacted, requiring another rewrite and the publication of our fourth edition. As we go to press, there are many major areas of our immigration law that are undergoing close scrutiny by our government and various public interest groups.

This revised fourth edition has been updated and covers, in detail, more categories of visas and related matters. **Immigration Made Simple** has, once again, been developed as an easy to use reference for foreign nationals who currently live and work in the United States, and for those wishing to do so in the near future. The book should also continue to be of considerable value to those who work with foreign students; corporate personnel working with foreign employees; business managers; the legal profession and its support staff; and others who have occasion to work with our U.S. Immigration process.

The order of the subject matter is intended to be useful. I start by defining some frequently used terms. The sections that follow describe the most common categories of temporary and permanent immigration categories, give examples, and explain how to go about obtaining these visas. I have tried to make these sections as easy to understand as possible, which was a difficult task! The last section of the book will provide you with answers to some of the most commonly asked immigration questions. At the end of the book, is an updated **Directory of Immigration Lawyers** to assist our readers in locating a qualified attorney. There are also several appendices, which contain information that I think you will find very helpful.

This edition of **Immigration Made Simple**, was once again written in collaboration with a very experienced immigration lawyer, Alan Lubiner, who has worked for the Immigration & Naturalization Service, and is currently in private practice in New Jersey. By collaborating with Alan, I am ensured a professional final product, and the reader gets the benefit of an "insiders" perspective.

Keep in mind that this book was not written to give legal advice, recommend solutions to complex immigration problems, nor to replace the service of Immigration lawyers. Many topics are not covered, including exclusion and deportation proceedings, political asylum applications and appeal procedures. My goal in making **Immigration Made Simple** available to you is very simple. After you read the chapters that follow, I hope that you will have a better understanding of the practical side of our immigration system and the options available to you, and that the book will serve as a helpful reference guide in the future.

Barbara Kimmel
President, Publisher and Co-Author

INTRODUCTION

The United States has, for generations, been called a "melting pot", a nation of immigrants. For over two hundred years, people from other countries have come to the United States to find safe haven from religious and political persecution, to seek economic opportunity and to reunite with family members. The ethnic and cultural diversity, the brains and talent, as well as the dreams and hopes that immigrants have brought to our country over the years are what have molded our national character and made the United States the super power that it is today.

In recent years. our immigration policy and our immigrants have come under attack from groups that would have us believe that immigrants are the root of all evil in our society. Major legislation has been proposed with the intention of sealing our borders. Various politicians and special interest groups seek a moratorium on immigration. Over the past two years sweeping changes in our immigration laws have been enacted that severely restrict the ability of our residents and citizens to reunite with their loved ones. Backlogs in quotas and harsh penalties have caused the breakup of families. Husbands are being separated from wives, parents from children, all in the name of "immigration reform".

The reality is that less than one million immigrants arrive in the United States each year. Undocumented immigrants constitute only one percent of the total U.S. population. Most immigrants are coming to join immediate family members, while a relatively small number are coming to jobs where the employer has demonstrated the inability to find U.S. workers.

The extremist groups would have us believe that immigrants take jobs away from Americans. Nothing could be further from the truth. Immigrant entrepreneurial spirit has been the backbone of American industry and today immigrants are likely to be self-employed and start new businesses.

Politicians, calling for welfare reform and for keeping immigrants off public assistance claim immigrants are a drain on the U.S. economy. Again, rhetoric that has no basis in fact. Immigrants must prove that they have the ability to sustain themselves or they will not be allowed in the U.S. They are barred from any means tested programs for at least two years and because of recent legislation will be so barred for five years. Their sponsors, who must file an affidavit of support with the U.S. government, are now held to their promise of support by a binding contract.

Immigrants permeate the very fabric of America. They are our parents, grandparents, teachers, friends, doctors, lawyers, sports heroes, actors, cooks, waiters, baby-sitters, store owners, and yes, even our politicians. They are an integral part of America and what makes the United States the greatest country in the world.

Alan Lubiner
Immigration Attorney and Co-Author

1 DEFINITIONS

Citizens of other countries who come to the U.S., and individuals who have occasion to work with the U.S. visa process, should become familiar with immigration "jargon". You will encounter the following terms frequently, and so it is best to know what they mean before reading further.

■ *Antiterrorism and Effective Death Penalty Act (AEDPA):* the Act signed into law by President Clinton on April 24, 1996 included sweeping new reforms, expanding the definition of aggravated felony and severely restricting the ability of an alien to obtain any form of waiver.

■ *Alien:* a person who is not a citizen or a national of the U.S. The term refers to all foreign nationals in the U.S., whether they are here temporarily or with permanent resident status. Although the term may seem strange to you, it is frequently used in the immigration field generally, and therefore in this book.

■ *Beneficiary:* an alien who is the recipient of an application filed on their behalf by another individual or organization.

■ *Citizen:* a person who owes their loyalty to, either through birth or naturalization, the protection of a given country. A permanent resident of the United States is not a United States citizen.

■ *Form I-9-Employment Eligibility Verification:* an employment form that must be completed by every employer and employee to verify the employee's identity and right to work in the U.S.

■ *Form I-94- Arrival and Departure Record:* a document that is issued to every alien who enters the United States for a temporary stay and who is officially inspected by a U.S. Immigration Officer. This document is stapled in the passport and indicates the amount of time the individual can initially remain in the United States. Form I-94W will be issued to individuals entering the U.S. under the Visa Waiver Pilot Program.

■ *Green Card:* a slang term for the identity document or alien registration receipt card issued to permanent resident (immigrant) aliens. The card includes the alien's photograph, fingerprint and signature. At one time the Form I-551 identity card was green, which is how it derived its name.

■ *Immigrant:* an alien who comes to the United States to live permanently.

■ *Immigration Act of 1990 (IMMACT 90):* the Act signed into law by President Bush on November 29, 1990. It represented the most extensive change in all areas of immigration in over fifty years.

■ *Illegal Immigration Reform and Immigrant Responsibility Act of 1996 (IIRAIRA):* the Act signed into law by President Clinton became effective on April 1, 1997. It made extensive changes to the immigration laws affecting the arrival of aliens, their treatment by the Immigration Court, and available forms of relief.

■ *Immigration and Naturalization Service (INS):* a branch of the United States Department of Justice. The INS is responsible for admitting foreign nationals into the U.S., and processing all immigration and naturalization related applications made by, or on behalf of, foreign nationals. The INS maintains offices throughout the U.S. and in several foreign countries. (See Appendix B for a complete list of INS offices in the U.S.)

■ *NAFTA:* North American Free Trade Agreement, approved by Congress in 1993. The Agreement liberalizes trade between the United States, Canada and Mexico, and contains immigration provisions described in Chapter 4.

■ *Naturalization:* a process by which permanent resident aliens can convert their status to U.S. citizenship. Naturalization permits the individual to obtain a U.S. passport and to vote in U.S. elections.

■ *Nonimmigrant:* an alien who comes to the U.S. for a temporary stay.

■ *Passport:* a document issued by a government that identifies the holder and his citizenship, and permits that individual to travel abroad.

■ *Permanent Resident:* a person who has the right to live permanently in the U.S. Individuals are given alien registration cards upon approval of their application for permanent residence and are thereafter called permanent resident aliens. Immigrant is another name for permanent resident alien. A permanent resident is not a U.S. citizen.

■ *Petitioner:* the employer or individual that is filing an application on behalf of an alien.

■ *Port of Entry:* a port or place where an alien may apply for admission into the U.S.

■ *United States Consulate:* the foreign headquarters of the U.S. Consul and his or her staff. These offices, which are located in most countries, have many departments, including a visa section that processes temporary and permanent visas for foreigners coming to the U.S.

■ *Visa:* the document need for travel to the U.S. Individuals planning to travel to the U.S. from many countries as nonimmigrants (for a temporary stay) must apply for entry permission at an American Consulate outside the U.S. A stamp (visa) placed in his or her passport, permits that individual to board a vessel to the U.S. The stamp contains the visa category, a visa number, the location and date that it was issued, the number of entries into the United States for which it can be used, and the expiration date.

2 TEMPORARY VISAS

The U.S. immigration system is divided into two groups, nonimmigrant and immigrant. Nonimmigrant categories are for individuals who wish to come to the U.S. for a temporary stay, for vacation, to attend school, or for temporary employment. Immigrant categories are for those who wish to live permanently in the U.S.

This chapter covers temporary or nonimmigrant visa categories. It first explains each nonimmigrant classification, then describes processing procedures, and the documents that are required in order to apply for each visa. The reference chart at the end of the chapter lists all of the nonimmigrant visas, and indicates to whom they apply.

CATEGORIES OF TEMPORARY OR NONIMMIGRANT VISAS

Nonimmigrant visas are issued to individuals who wish to enter the United States for a temporary period of time ranging from one day to several years. In most cases, an individual must establish that he or she has a residence in his home country that will not be abandoned. Some people may be eligible for many different types of visas, while others may not qualify at all. There is a long list of reasons why certain individuals cannot be admitted into the U.S. Examples of such reasons are certain mental or physical disorders, criminal convictions, drug or alcohol addiction, prostitution, etc. Waivers are available in some cases. Further information should be obtained from a knowledgeable professional.

A-1, A-2, A-3. Foreign Government Officials

"A" visas are granted to foreign government officials, their families and servants. This includes ambassadors, public ministers, diplomats or consular officers who are assigned to represent their country in the U.S. The processing of these visas is usually handled directly by the sponsoring organization.

B-1. Temporary Business Visitor

B-1 visas are granted to foreign business people coming to the U.S. for their foreign employer. They are also issued to self employed individuals who need to conduct business, such as attending meetings or conferences, meeting customers, or negotiating contracts. The alien must continue to be paid by the foreign employer, and must maintain a residence abroad that he or she has no intention of abandoning. The B-1 visa holder cannot be "employed" in the United States or earn money directly from U.S. sources.

In some countries the American Consulate will issue a multiple entry B-1 visa so that the alien may enter the U.S several times using the same visa. In other countries, only a single entry visa will be issued. The validity date of the visa will vary depending upon the country in which the visa is issued. Upon entry into the U.S., the B-1 visitor is usually admitted for the length of time need to complete the purpose of the trip, generally for three months, but not exceeding six months.

The visa application is made to the appropriate American Consulate abroad. It consists of:

---

1. Optional Form- 156 Nonimmigrant Visa Application, which can be obtained at the American Consulate
2. Passport photograph
3. Letter from the foreign employer explaining the reason for the visit to the United States
4. Valid passport or travel document.

B-2. Temporary Visitor for Pleasure

B-2 visas are issued to people coming to the U.S. to visit friends or relatives, to vacation or to accompany a B-1 visa holder as described above.

In most cases, the American Consulate will require evidence of the nature of the trip, as well as proof that the applicant intends to return to the home country. Sometimes an invitation from a friend or relative in the U.S., proof of residence and employment abroad, and other evidence of permanent ties outside the U.S. can help to establish the "intention to return". The applicant should also provide a round-trip airline ticket, and proof that he or she has enough money available for the duration of the trip, such as bank statements or credit cards. The B-2 visa can be issued for multiple trips.

Upon entry to the U.S., the alien is generally admitted for six months. Until a few years ago, B-2 visitors were admitted for the length of time of their intended visit, not to exceed six months. The INS then started admitting B-2 visitors automatically for six months to eliminate extension requests and save time and paperwork.

The application must be made at an American Consulate. It consists of:

---

1. Optional Form 156- Nonimmigrant Visa Application
2. Passport photograph
3. Valid passport or travel document.

If a visitor can show a good reason for needing to stay in the U.S. beyond the initial six months, the alien can apply for one six month extension. The application is filed with the INS Service Center having jurisdiction over the applicant's temporary residence in the U.S. It consists of:

1. Form I-539- Application to Extend/Change Nonimmigrant Status
2. Letter of explanation and any documentation in support of the extension request showing why it is requested
3. Copy of return transportation ticket
4. Copy of Form I-94
5. Filing fee of $75.00.

Chapter 3 covers the "Visa Waiver Pilot Program", which allows citizens from many countries to travel to the U.S. as business or pleasure visitors without having to apply for a B-1 or B-2 visa at an American Consulate.

C. Transit Visas and Transit Without Visa

"C" visas are transit visas. They are used by people who are traveling through the U.S. to a final destination outside the U.S. People admitted in "C" status may remain in the U.S. for a maximum of twenty nine days. A "transit" alien may not apply for change of status to any other nonimmigrant category except "G", and may not apply for an extension of temporary stay.

Some people who are in transit through the U.S. do not have visas. Transit without visa or TWOV is reserved for those who are applying for admission to the U.S. to travel on to another country. Someone flying into the U.S. who has a confirmed reservation, within a specified time period, to catch a connecting flight to another country will be admitted as TWOV. Aliens in TWOV status are not permitted to leave the airline terminal. Application for TWOV status can only be made at certain designated U.S. ports of entry.

D. Crewmen of Aircraft or Sea Vessels

This visa is used by aliens who are applying for admission into the U.S. as members of a foreign vessel's crew such as flight attendants on foreign owned airlines, or crewmen on foreign owned ships. Usually the foreign vessel personnel will make the arrangements for "D" visa issuance. Many crewmen have both "C" and "D" visas. They use the "C" visas for the purpose of entering the U.S. to "join" their vessel.

There is no derivative classification for the spouse or children of crewmen. They are classified as B-2 visitors if coming solely to the U.S. to accompany the principal alien.

15

E-1 & E-2. Treaty Trader or Investor

E-1 visas are available to Treaty Traders, while E-2 visas are available to Treaty Investors. Both categories require that the United States maintain treaties of commerce and navigation with the foreign country, allowing for trade and/or investment in the United States. Aliens applying for either type of "E" visa must have the same citizenship of the country that maintains the treaty with the United States. The following is a current list of countries that have such treaties. Countries followed by one asterisk (*) have treaty trader provisions, allowing only for issuance of E-1 visas. Countries followed by two asterisks (**) have treaty investor provisions, allowing only for issuance of E-2 visas. Countries with no asterisk(s) maintain both treaty trader <u>and</u> treaty investor provisions, and issue both types of visas.

Argentina
Armenia **
Australia
Austria
Bangladesh **
Belgium
Bolivia *
Brunei * (Borneo)
Bulgaria **
Cameroon **
Canada
China (Taiwan)
Colombia
The Congo **
Costa Rica
Czech Republic **
Denmark *
Egypt **
Estonia *
Ethiopia
Finland
France
Germany
Greece *
Grenada **
Honduras
Iran (may be affected by embargo)
Ireland
Israel *
Italy
Japan
Kazakhstan **
Korea
Kyrgyzstan **

Latvia *
Liberia
Luxembourg **
Mexico
Morocco
Netherlands
Norway
Oman
Pakistan
Panama **
Paraguay
Philippines
Poland **
Romania **
Senegal **
Slovak Republic **
Spain
Sri Lanka **
Suriname
Sweden
Switzerland
Taiwan
Thailand
Togo
Tunisia **
Turkey
United Kingdom
Yugoslavia
Zaire **

Bilateral investment treaties signed in 1992 and 1993 respectively will soon authorize E-2 classification for nationals of Ecuador and Russia: In 1996 the United States approved treaties with nine countries: Albania, Belarus, Estonia, Georgia, Jamaica, Latvia, Mongolia, Trinidad and Tobago, and Ukraine. Once ratified by the United States and each country involved, these treaties should take effect about thirty days after the countries exchange instruments of ratification. They are for E-2 classification only.

1) Treaty Traders

Treaty traders enter the United States for the sole purpose of carrying on substantial trade. Many are self-employed people whose trade with the United States accounts for more than 50% of their total volume of trade. The definition of "trade" has been expanded over the years to encompass not only goods and services but also trade in technology. The treaty trader may also be an employee of a company that qualifies for treaty trader status, but the employment must be in a position that is either executive or supervisory in nature, or one involving essential skills.

2) Treaty Investors

Treaty investors enter the United States to make a substantial investment in a U.S. business, and to direct and develop the business. There is no specific dollar amount needed to qualify for this type of visa. The investment must, however, be substantial in terms of the total investment in the enterprise. The investment must be in a business that generates active income, rather than passive income such as rental property, and the business must be at least 50% owned by nationals of the treaty country, (that being the same country of nationality as the alien). Treaty investors may also be employees of a company that qualifies for treaty investor status, but like the treaty trader, the employment must be in a position that is either executive or supervisory, or one that involves essential skills.

Rules involving "E" visas are very complex, and there are ramifications of some treaties, including certain rules under NAFTA (the North American Free Trade Agreement) that affect the procedures for entry into the United States. (See Chapter 4). Those seeking "E" visa status should speak with an experienced immigration practitioner.

F-1. Student

F-1 visas are available to aliens coming temporarily to the United States to attend school. The applicant must plan to pursue a full time program of academic study at an educational institution that is authorized by the Immigration and Naturalization Service to enroll foreign students. The student must have a home in a foreign country to which he or she will return after completion of studies. In addition, he or she must be proficient in the

English language, and have sufficient funds available for his or her support during studies in the U.S.

F-1 status is not available to aliens who wish to attend a public elementary school or a public adult education program. Entry into the U.S. to attend a public secondary school is also prohibited unless the total period in F-1 status does not exceed one year and the alien reimburses the school for the costs of providing education. Any alien who violates this provision is barred from admission to the United States for a period of five years.

The visa application consists of:

1. Optional Form 156- Nonimmigrant Visa Application
2. Form I-20 A-B/I-20ID - Certificate of Eligibility of Nonimmigrant (F-1) Student Status- for Academic and Language Students- issued by the sponsoring school
3. Passport photographs
4. Proof that the applicant has enough money to pay all school related expenses and to support himself or herself during the program, as indicated on Form I-20A-B/I-20ID
5. Proof that the applicant has a home abroad that is not being abandoned, and that the student plans to leave the U.S. when the program is completed
6. Valid passport or travel document.

Note: Student applicants who have not yet made a final decision on the school they wish to attend, and want to come to the U.S. to visit the schools to make a final selection, may apply for a "B-2" visitor's visa. The applicant must disclose, to the American Consulate, the reason for their trip. The Consular Officer should note "prospective student" on the visa. Prospective students must apply to the INS for a change of visa status after they have made their final school selection.

Qualified students who wish to enter the U.S. more than ninety days before their school's starting date, can apply for a B-2 visa with the understanding that they will file with the Immigration & Naturalization Service to change to F-1 status prior to commencing studies.

A Note of Caution: In the above instances, after approval of a change of status, the student will not have a student "visa", only student status in the U.S. If the student leaves the U.S., he or she must apply for an F-1 visa at an American Consulate before reentering the United States as a student.

The visa is usually granted for the period of time in which the student is pursuing a full time course of study, including engaging in practical training, plus sixty days to prepare for departure from the U.S. This is referred to as "duration of status" or "D/S". The American Consular Official will sometimes write the school's name on the visa. The I-20A-B/I-20ID should be returned to the student, who should subsequently present it to the INS official at the point of entry into the U.S. The INS officer will then issue Form I-94, write the admission number from Form I-94 on Form I-20, and return the "student part" of Form I-20 (I-20ID). The INS will then forward the school's copy of Form I-20 to the INS processing center, which will then send it back to the school as evidence of the student's admission in F-1 status.

Under normal conditions, the student is not required to apply for extension of stay in the U.S., as long as he or she is a full time student, and will complete the course of study within the time indicated on Form I-20. Spouses and minor children can be granted F-2 visas, which are not valid for employment.

Students who will remain in one educational level for an extended period of time, or remain in student status for eight consecutive years should check with the DSO about extending their stay.

A student who is in F-1 status can leave the U.S. for up to five months and be readmitted in student status as long as:

1. He or she has a current I-20ID endorsed by the Designated School Official (DSO), who is often the Foreign Student Adviser, or
2. A new Form I-20A-B if the student's program is changing (such as a change in major, advancement to a higher level of study, or an intended school transfer)
3. The student must also have a valid student visa and a passport valid for at least six months.

Students pursuing a full time course of study can transfer from one school to another within the U.S without requiring prior INS approval. The procedure is as follows:

✔ Notify the DSO of plans to transfer

✔ Complete enrollment in the new school without any break between semesters

✔ Obtain Form I-20A-B from the new school. Follow instructions from the new Foreign Student Adviser for completing certain items on Form I-20A-B/I20ID, and return the form to the DSO at the new school within fifteen days after classes begin

✔ The DSO will then add the name of the old school to Form I-20A-B/I20ID, write the student's admission number on the form, indicate that the transfer was completed, sign it and return the student's copy. The DSO will also send a copy of the new form to the old school, and submit the form to the INS data processing center within thirty days.

A student who is not pursuing a full time course of study, and who wants to transfer to another school, must apply to the INS for reinstatement to student status. The application for reinstatement must include Form I-20A-B from the new school. If reinstated, the student may attend the new school without a transfer of paperwork.

A student who has violated status may be reinstated if the student can establish that the violation resulted from circumstances beyond his or her control, or that he or she would suffer extreme hardship if not reinstated. The decision, which is made by the INS, is completely discretionary. The student must make a formal request for reinstatement on Form I-539, accompanied by Form I-20A-B/I20ID. The applicant must be pursuing or intending to pursue a full course of study; must not have worked without authorization and; must not be deportable on any other ground.

Note of Caution: A student who has violated his status, even for one day, may be ineligible for adjustment of status if Section 245(i) of the Immigration and Nationality Act is not renewed. See Chapter Six for further details.

Generally, foreign students are not allowed to work in the United States. As noted earlier, one of the requirements for a student visa is that the student prove that enough funds are available to pay for his or her education and support for the duration of studies. However, there <u>are</u> three ways that students can work while in F-1 status. They are:

1. **On campus employment**
2. **Practical training** - includes curricular practical training and optional practical training
3. **Off campus employment**.

1. On campus employment- this applies to students who will work in an on-campus establishment such as the cafeteria or bookstore. It may also apply to "off campus" sites which are "affiliated educationally" with the school. The employment must be an "integral part" of the educational program, and cannot exceed twenty hours per week while school is in session. Full time, on campus employment is allowed during summer vacations and holidays when school is not open.

2. Practical training- this is divided into two categories:

A. Curricular Practical Training:

This applies to training as part of an established curriculum during the student's regular course of study. It includes work/study programs, cooperative educational programs, or internships offered by employers through agreements with the school. In order to qualify for curricular practical training, the student must have been lawfully enrolled in school, on a full-time basis, for at least nine consecutive months (exception for students of some graduate study programs which require immediate curricular practical training). The position must be directly related to the student's major field of study.

The application is made as follows:

✔ Student submits Form I-538 and I-20ID to the DSO

✔ DSO certifies the curricular practical training on Form I-538, and on Form I-20ID the DSO certifies the dates and location of the student's curricular practical training

✔ DSO signs and dates the I-20ID and returns it to the student

✔ DSO sends the school certification on Form I-538 to the INS data processing center.

Note: Students who have participated in one year or more of full-time curricular practical training may not participate in practical training after completion of their course of study.

B. *Optional Practical Training* (either before or after completion of studies):

Optional practical training can only be authorized in an occupation that is directly related to the student's major. A student may qualify after he or she has been lawfully enrolled in school, on a full time basis, for at least nine consecutive months. The period of optional practical training, both before and after studies, cannot exceed twelve months. Optional practical training is available during the following four periods:

1) During vacation periods while school is not in session, if the student is currently enrolled and intends to register for the next term
2) While school is in session, not to exceed twenty hours per week
3) After completion of all course requirements
4) After completion of the entire course of study.

All optional practical training must be completed within fourteen months after the completion of study. This application is made as follows:

✔ Student submits Form I-538 and I-20ID to the DSO

✔ DSO certifies on Form I-538 that the employment is directly related to the student's area of study and within his or her educational level

✔ DSO signs and dates the I-20ID to show that the training is recommended, indicates dates of practical training and whether full or part-time, and returns the I-20ID to the student
continued on next page

21

✔ DSO sends the school certification on Form I-538 to the INS data processing center.

The student must then apply to the INS office for an employment authorization document (EAD) by submitting the following:

---

1. Form I-765-Application for Employment Authorization
2. Form I-20ID - endorsed by the DSO
3. Applicable filing fee
4. Copy of Form I-94
5. (Some INS offices need a special fingerprint card and photos).

Note: Some INS offices require that applications be mailed while others accept in-person applications

---

Once the application for optional practical training has been approved, the INS will return Form I-20ID and issue an Employment Authorization Document (EAD). The student cannot commence employment until the EAD is received. The INS hopes to be able to approve these applications very quickly. Again, training must be completed within fourteen months of finishing studies.

Note: Students in English language training programs are not eligible for practical training.

3. Off-campus Employment (due to urgent financial need)

A student can apply for part-time (no more than twenty hours per week while school is in session) off-campus employment after having been in good academic standing for at least one year. The request must be based upon severe economic hardship, caused by unforeseen circumstances beyond the student's control. Examples include: loss of financial aid, loss of on-campus employment, substantial fluctuations in the value of currency, inordinate increases in tuition and/or living expenses, unexpected changes in the financial condition of the student's source of support, or unexpected medical bills.

The procedure for obtaining work authorization is as follows:

✔ Student completes his or her portion of Form I-538 and submits it with the I-20ID to the DSO

✔ DSO certifies on Form I-538 that the off-campus employment is warranted and submits Form I-538 to the INS data processing center.

continued on next page

✔ Student submits Form I-765, the I-20ID, Form I-94, a special fingerprint card, two photographs, the required fee, and evidence in support of the application to the INS service center having jurisidiction over his place of residence

✔ If granted, the Employment Authorization Document will be issued for one year intervals up to the date the student is expected to complete studies, as long as the student maintains status, and is in good academic standing

✔ The student may not begin work until the EAD has been issued.

There are two other types of visas for students, the M-1 and the J-1, which are discussed in this chapter. The requirements and regulations are different for each one. Make sure you choose the student status that will offer you the most benefits.

Note: Prior to September 30, 1996, a Pilot Off-Campus Employment Program was in existence. The Immigration Act of 1990 established a trial program to allow foreign students to work off-campus for employers who had received prior approval (called a Labor Attestation) from the Department of Labor (DOL), and from the student's school. This was referred to as the "McDonald's Provision". The program ran from October 1, 1991 to September 30, 1996. It has not been renewed.

G-1 thru G-5. Representatives to International Organizations

Similar to "A" visas, "G" visas are issued to representatives of international organizations like the United Nations and World Bank, as well as missions. Family members, staff and servants are also eligible for this category. The application is usually handled directly by the sponsoring organization.

H. Temporary Worker

This is a very broad visa category and covers several different types of temporary workers including: aliens in specialty occupations; farm workers and other temporary nonagricultural workers; trainees; and family members of "H" visa holders. The categories will be described in numerical order.

H-1A. Nurses

This visa was previously available to foreign nurses. It went into effect in December, 1989, because of a shortage of qualified nurses in the U.S. In addition to separating nurses into their own "H" category, the Immigration Nursing Relief Act of 1989 (INRA) also provided for certain nurses already in the U.S. to convert to permanent residence. Finally, INRA set up a five year program, commencing September 1, 1990, where the petitioning health care facility provided certain documentation to the Department of Labor. This program expired on September 1, 1995. After September 1, 1995 nurses already in H-1A status are permitted to remain in that status and may extend their stay to a maximum of six years. Nurses applying after September 1, 1995 are now included in the H-1B category, and must meet all H-1B criteria to be eligible.

H-1B. Aliens in Specialty Occupations

"Aliens in specialty occupations" (professionals) who have a temporary job offer in the U.S. may be eligible for H-1B classification. Note that artists and entertainers were removed from this category under the Immigration Act of 1990. Other major changes in this category include requiring a labor condition attestation, which must be approved by the Department of Labor; extension of the maximum period of stay in H-1B status from five to six years; and the adoption of an annual 65,000 H-1B numerical ceiling.

The INS definition of "specialty occupation" is: "one that requires theoretical and practical application of a body of highly specialized knowledge; and the attainment of a bachelor's degree or higher in the specific specialty as the minimum for entry into the occupation in the U.S."

As indicated above, prospective H-1B employers are required to file a labor attestation, Form ETA-9035 "Labor Condition Application for H-1B Nonimmigrants", with the Employment and Training Administration of the U.S. Department of Labor.

The INS regulations require the employer to prove the following:

✔ That H-1B nonimmigrants and other workers in similar jobs will be paid the actual wage for the occupation at the place of employment, or the prevailing wage level for the occupation in that geographic area, which ever one is higher. The employer can use either a State Employment Service (SESA) determination or a wage survey, and indicate the source of the prevailing wage information

✔ That the employment of H-1B workers will not impact adversely on the working conditions of other people similarly employed in that geographic area

✔ That there is no strike, lockout or work stoppage in the occupation at the place of intended employment

continued on next page

24

✔ That notice of the filing of the H-1B application has been given to workers at the place of intended employment through a bargaining representative, or if not applicable, through a posted notice of the filing at the place of intended employment.

A visa petition must first be filed with the INS Regional Service Center in the U.S. by the company that is offering the temporary employment. The application consists of:

1. An approved Labor Attestation from the Department of Labor
2. Form I-129-Petition for a Nonimmigrant Worker
3. Proof of the alien's academic qualifications and professional experience - university degrees, letters of reference, etc.
4. A letter from the company describing the company, the temporary job to be filled, including why it requires at least a bachelor's degree, and why the alien is particularly qualified, as well as a statement that the employer will pay for the alien's return trip abroad if the employment is terminated before the authorized stay expires
5. The applicable filing fee.

The INS will review the application and issue an approval notice to the company. The INS should also cable notice of approval to the American Consulate where the alien will apply for the visa. Approval can be granted for an initial period of three years. Extensions of H-1 status can routinely be obtained for an additional three years (maximum stay in H-1 status is six years). The INS processing time for H-1 petitions varies, but is usually not more than one to two months.

Once the company receives the approval notice, the bottom half should be forwarded to the alien so that visa application can be made at the American Consulate. This consists of:

1. Optional Form 156- Nonimmigrant Visa Application
2. Passport photograph
3. Original H-1B approval notice receipt issued by the INS.

The alien should obtain a complete copy of the H-1 application prior to applying for the visa. When the visa application is made, the alien should be able to affirm that he or she will remain in the U.S. temporarily. The visa is normally granted for three years. Spouses and minor children are issued H-4 visas, which are not valid for employment in the U.S.

25

H-2. Temporary Worker in Field Where U.S. Workers are in Short Supply

This category is divided into two groups:

H-2A. Temporary agricultural service workers

H-2B. Other workers who will be performing temporary services of labor in which U.S. workers are not available, including some seasonal jobs, certain child care situations, and individuals who will be training U.S. workers. The new immigration regulations include a 66,000 annual ceiling on issuance of H-2B visas.

Processing of H-2 applications is complex.

✔ The employer must first file a request with the local office of the State Employment Service (using Form ETA 750, Part A) for a temporary labor certification

✔ The State Employment Service will then issue instructions to the prospective employer regarding attempts to recruit U.S. workers, including advertising the job opening in a newspaper or trade publication, depending on the nature of the job

✔ Assuming approval after complying with the requirements, the Department of Labor will issue a certification.

An application is then filed with the INS, consisting of:

```
1. Department of Labor Certification
2. Form I-129-Petition for Nonimmigrant Worker
3. A letter from the prospective employer describing the job
   and including a statement that the employer will pay for
   the alien's return transportation abroad
4. Evidence of the alien's qualifications
5. Applicable filing fee.
```

Once the application is approved, the process for obtaining the visa is similar to that for the H-1, and families can be granted H-4 visas. H-2 visas are issued in one year increments, with maximum duration of three years.

H-3. Temporary Trainee

The H-3 visa is available to individuals who will participate, within a business in the U.S., in a formal training program that does not involve productive work (productive work can only be incidental to the training). The procedure for applying to the INS is similar to the H-1 process described above;

however, a labor attestation is not required. The prospective employer's petition to the INS must be accompanied by a written description of the formal training program, including details such as: the duration of the different phases of the training including classroom work; the instructors who will provide the training; reading and course work required during the training; why the training is not available in the alien's own country; and the position that the alien will fill abroad at the end of the training in the U.S.

The visa is usually granted for the duration of the training program, or for up to two years. Accompanying family members are issued H-4 visas.

INS regulations also allow for an H-3 "Special Education Exchange Visitor Program" for nonimmigrants coming to the U.S. to participate in a special education training program that provides practical training and experience in the education of children with physical, mental or emotional handicaps. Only fifty people per year are eligible, with a limit of stay in the U.S. of eighteen months.

I. Representatives of Information Media

This visa category is reserved for aliens who are coming to the U.S. temporarily to work on behalf of a foreign information media such as a foreign newspaper or television station. "I" visa holders are admitted to the U.S. for the duration of their employment. So few visas are issued in this category that it will not be discussed further in this book.

J-1. Exchange Visitor

J-1 visas are available to aliens who will be participating in an Exchange Visitor Program including experts, foreign students, industrial and business trainees, "international visitors", medical interns and residents, and scholars. Exchange Visitor Programs are approved and administered by the United States Information Agency (USIA).

The Exchange Visitor Program was developed, in part, to allow aliens to pursue education, training or research, or to teach in the U.S. Many large companies and educational institutions participate. Foreign medical graduates who wish to study further or train in the U.S. may want to first contact the Educational Commission for Foreign Medical Graduates (ECFMG) located in Philadelphia, Pennsylvania. In recent years, the USIA has also approved several programs that are designed to enable au pairs to come to the U.S. to reside with American families for temporary periods.

Sponsors of J-1 programs can be:

- An existing U.S. agency or organization
- A recognized international agency or organization having U.S. membership and offices
- A reputable organization which is a "citizen of the United States".

Citizen of the United States is defined as either:

1. An individual U.S. citizen

2. A partnership of which a majority of the partners are U.S. citizens

3. A corporation or other legal entity, which has its principal place of business in the United States, and either its shares are publicly traded on a U.S. stock exchange or a majority of its officers, directors and shareholders are U.S. citizens.

4. A non-profit legal entity in the U.S. which is qualified as tax-exempt, has its principal place of business in the U.S. and a majority of its officers and directors are U.S. citizens or

5. An accredited college, university or other institution of higher learning created under U.S. law.

Foreign nationals who wish to apply for J-1 visas should proceed with caution, because many aliens must return to their home country for two years after they complete their stay in J-1 status. These include:

1. Individuals who receive any sort of government funding to participate in the J-1 program in the U.S.
2. Aliens receiving graduate medical training in the U.S., such as residents and interns
3. Aliens who are nationals of a country in which a *skills list* exists.

The skills list indicates occupations for which the foreign country's local workers are in short supply. The Department of State has compiled this list in cooperation with each foreign government. For example, the Brazilian government may have concluded that not enough Brazilians are qualified engineers. Therefore, if a Brazilian citizen comes to the United States with a J-1 visa to pursue a course of study in engineering, he or she is required to return to Brazil for two years after completing the J-1 program in the U.S. This is known as the "two year foreign residence requirement." In some cases this two year requirement can be waived at the end of the program, but it is a difficult procedure, and with no guarantees of approval.

When the alien has been accepted into a J-1 program, the sponsoring organization will issue Form IAP-66 (Certificate of Eligibility for Exchange Visitor J-1 Status) to the foreign national. The visa application made to the American Consulate consists of:

1. Optional Form 156- Nonimmigrant Visa Application
2. Passport photograph
3. Form IAP-66
4. Valid passport or travel document.

The J-1 visa is usually issued to coincide with the length of the J-1 program. Some J-1 visas can be renewed while others are limited to fixed periods of stay. Spouses and minor children are granted J-2 visas. They may accept employment by applying to the INS for permission to work on Form I-765. Employment permission can be granted for up to four years, or the duration of the J-1's IAP-66/I-94, whichever is shorter.

K. Fiancé or Fiancee of U.S. Citizen

This category is available to aliens who are outside the U.S. and are engaged to be married to a U.S. citizen. The petitioner and the beneficiary must have met in person within the past two years. The U.S. citizen must file the following documents with the INS:

1. Form I-129F-Petition for Alien Fiancé
2. Proof of U.S. citizenship of petitioner
3. Proof of termination of prior marriages for both parties, if applicable
4. Evidence that the two parties have physically met within the past two years
5. Statements from both parties that they plan to marry within 90 days of the alien's admission to the U.S. and evidence as to this intent
6. Two color photos of the U.S. citizen, and two of the fiancé(e) taken within 30 days
7. Applicable filing fee.

The INS will approve the petition and forward it to the U.S. Consulate where the fiancé(e) will apply for the visa, after complying with the instructions of the Consul. Once the alien is granted the K-1 visa and enters the U.S., the marriage must occur within 90 days. After the marriage, the alien can file Form I-485- Application to Register Permanent Residence with the INS to convert from K-1 to conditional residence (See Chapter on Permanent Residence for procedures on filing Form I-485). Unmarried minor children can accompany the fiancé(e) to the U.S. in "K" status.

L-1. Intracompany Transferee

L-1 visas are granted to aliens who have worked for a company abroad, as executives, managers, or in a specialized knowledge capacity, for a total of one year within the immediately preceding three years. The INS has very strict definitions of "managerial, executive and specialized knowledge". The alien must be transferred, for a temporary assignment, to a branch office, subsidiary or affiliate company in the U.S. in an executive, managerial or specialized knowledge capacity. The employer in the U.S. must initiate a petition with the INS.

The L-1 petition consists of:

> 1. Form I-129- Petition for A Nonimmigrant Worker and "L" classification supplement
> 2. A letter describing the alien's current job, held for the past year abroad, and the anticipated job in the U.S. It should include details of the executive, managerial or specialized knowledge features of both positions
> 3. Proof that the alien has been employed abroad by the foreign company for at least one year
> 4. Proof that the foreign and U.S. companies are related
> 5. Applicable filing fee.

The INS will issue a notice of approval to the prospective U.S. employer, usually within thirty days. The visa application process from this point forward is the same as that described for the H-1B.

The initial petition can be approved for up to three years with extensions granted in two year increments, up to seven years in total for executives and managers. Specialized knowledge L-1 aliens are only eligible for a total of five years in this visa category. Spouses and minor children are granted L-2 visas, which are not valid for work purposes.

If the U.S. company has just started operating, the application rules are different. The INS may ask to see more documents, the petition may only be approved for one year, and the subsequent visa will only be issued for one year. Should the employer need to renew the status of the L-1 alien at the end of the first year, the U.S. company will be required to prove to the INS that the new operation is growing. If this proof is available, extensions of stay can also be granted, as described above.

Employers are also entitled to apply to the INS for approval of an L-1 "blanket" petition, which eases the application process each time the employer wants to transfer an alien. In order to qualify for this program, the employer must be able to meet certain criteria. Included in these are:

1. That the employer must have had at least ten L-1 approvals within the past twelve months <u>or</u>
2. Have sales of over $25 million <u>or</u>
3. Employ at least 1000 people.
4. Have proof of affiliation between the U.S. and foreign branches of the company <u>and</u>
5. Have proof that the U.S. company has been doing business for at least a year.

The documentation required for L-1 blanket approval is extensive but can benefit the employer in saving time on international transfer paperwork.

M-1. Student

M-1 status is similar to F-1 status. This visa category has been in effect since 1982 and is designed for students who wish to pursue vocational or other recognized <u>nonacademic</u> educational programs. This does not include English language programs. The application process is similar to that for F-1 students in that the school issues Form I-20MN to the student. The visa application at the American Consulate consists of:

1. Optional Form 156- Nonimmigrant Visa Application
2. Form I-20M-N- Certificate of Eligibility for Nonimmigrant (M-1) Student Status- completed by the student and the DSO
3. Passport photographs
4. Proof that the applicant has enough money to pay school related expenses and to support himself or herself during the program
5. Valid passport or travel document.

The visa may be granted for the length of the course of study shown on Form I-20M. The I-20M-N should be returned to the student by the Consular official. The student should present it to the INS official when entering the U.S. The INS officer will return the student's part of the Form and issue Form I-94. The INS will also forward Form I-20M-N to the INS processing center, which will then send Form I-20N to the sponsoring school. Aliens holding M-1 visas are not permitted to work. Spouses and minor children can be granted M-2 visas, which are not valid for employment.

Students can transfer from one school to another within the U.S. after spending six months in valid M-1 status, and assuming he or she is financially able to continue to attend school. The procedure is as follows:

✔ Student completes Form I-538- Application by Nonimmigrant Student for Extension of Stay, and attaches Form I-20ID and Forms I-94 for him or herself and all family members

✔ Student obtains completed Form I-20M-N from the new sponsoring school and fills out the information required

✔ Student submits the application to the INS office having jurisdiction over the school the student last attended, consisting of:

---

1. Form I-538
2. Student's I-20ID
3. Form I-20M-N from the new school
4. Forms I-94 for student and family
5. Applicable filing fee

The student must wait for sixty days after filing the application for transfer, to start in the new program. If the application is approved it will be retroactive to the date of filing, and the student will be granted an extension of stay. The INS will return Form I-20ID and Form I-94. The extension period should coincide with the completion of the new program plus thirty days, or for one year, whichever is less. The INS officer will also endorse the name of the new school on the student's I-20N and will forward it along with Form I-20M to the INS data processing center. INS will record the change and send the form to the new school. If the application for transfer is denied, the student is considered to be out of status.

Students can also qualify for paid practical training upon completion of their program. The alien may only be employed in an occupation or vocation directly related to his or her course of study, as recommended by the DSO. The maximum amount of time for training will be one month for each four months of full time study, but not to exceed six months, plus thirty days to depart the U.S. The application process is as follows:

✔ Student completes his or her portion of Form I-538 and gives this to the DSO with Form I-20ID.

✔ DSO endorses the student's Form I-20ID for practical training and returns it to the student

✔ DSO completes the school's portion of Form I-538 and forwards it to the INS data processing center. On Form I-538 the DSO must certify that he or she recommends the proposed employment, that it is related to the student's course of study, and that this type of employment is not available in the student's home country.

The student must them apply to the INS service center for an employment authorization document (EAD). The application consists of:

1. Form I-765
2. Copy of Form I-94
3. Special fingerprint card
4. Photos
2. Form I-20ID endorsed for practical training by the DSO
3. Applicable filing fee.

The application must be submitted before the student's authorized stay expires and not more than sixty days before completing the course of study, nor more than thirty days after. The student cannot begin practical training until the INS approves the application, endorses the training on Form I-20ID and returns the EAD to the student.

N. NATO (not covered in this book)

O. Extraordinary Aliens

"O" aliens are those who have extraordinary ability in the sciences, arts, education, business or athletics. This includes those in the motion picture or television industries. The alien must have sustained national or international acclaim, or with regard to motion picture and television productions, have a demonstrated record of achievement.

The "O" alien must be entering the United States to continue work in the area of extraordinary ability, or for the purpose of accompanying and assisting in the artistic or athletic performance for a specific event. The alien must be an integral part of the actual performance, and possess skills and experience which cannot be duplicated by other individuals.

In the case of motion picture or television productions, the "O" applicant must have skills and experience which are critical, based on either a preexisting long-standing working relationship with the principal performer, or with respect to the specific production. This must be due to the fact that the significant production will take place both inside and outside the U.S., and the continuing participation of the alien is essential to the successful completion of the production.

Aliens of extraordinary ability, or extraordinary achievement in the motion picture or television industries are designated O-1. Aliens who accompany and assist O-1 aliens are classified O-2. This category is only available, however, for aliens who accompany or assist an O-1 alien in a specific athletic or artistic event. It is not available in the fields of education, science or business.

The spouse and children of O-1 or O-2 aliens are designated O-3. O-1 aliens do not need to have a residence abroad which they have no intention of abandoning, but O-2 aliens do have to maintain a residence abroad.

The standards for this visa category are very high. Television and movie artists must prove that they have a very high level of accomplishment, and that they have been recognized as outstanding, notable or leading. To show extraordinary ability in the sciences, business, education and athletics, applicants must document their recognition, with quality outweighing quantity.

"O" visas require a petition (Form I-129 with appropriate supplement) to be filed with the INS Regional Service Center having jurisdiction over the area in which the alien will be employed. The procedure is similar to that in H-1B cases. Established agents may file petitions (in lieu of employers) for an alien who is traditionally self-employed, or who plans to arrange short term employment with numerous employers. There are strict rules that agents must follow. Consult a professional for more information in this area.

The maximum period of validity of an approved "O" petition is three years. A petitioner may seek an extension in one year increments.

P. Outstanding Athletes, Artists and Entertainers

"P" visas are reserved for athletes, artists and certain entertainers who have achieved national or international recognition in their field. The standard is lower than for "O" visas but the scope of eligible services is more limited.

There are three subcategories:

> **P-1**. Members of entertainment groups, or individual athletes and members of athletic teams
>
> **P-2**. Artists or entertainers who are part of reciprocal international exchanges
>
> **P-3**. Artists or entertainers coming to perform in programs that are culturally unique.

Teachers and coaches, as well as performers, are now eligible for P-3 status, to encourage them to disseminate their knowledge. Aliens may also now be admitted for commercial or non-commercial performances. It is interesting to note that individual entertainers are not eligible for "P" visas, except for those participating in reciprocal exchanges, or performing in culturally unique shows.

Prior to the Immigration Act of 1990, athletes were admitted as visitors under a variety of situations. Now INS regulations grant P-1 status to professional athletes, while amateur athletes may still be granted B-1 status.

Like the "O" category, a petition is required. Family members are eligible for P-4 classification. All "P" nonimmigrants must seek to enter the United States temporarily, and are required to have a residence abroad that they do not intend to abandon. As with "O" petitions, an agent may file the petition. Individual athletes may be admitted for up to five years, and their stay may be extended for up to five years. The total period of stay for an individual athlete may not exceed ten years. All other "P" aliens can be admitted for up to one year, and their stay may be extended in increments of one year.

Q. International Cultural Exchange

This category was created to allow employer's like Disney to bring foreigners to the U.S. for temporary periods to work in places such as Epcot in Florida. This visa category applies to aliens coming to the U.S. for no more than fifteen months to participate in an international cultural exchange program. To qualify, the prospective employer must have been conducting business in the U.S. for at least two years, have at least five full-time U.S. workers, and offer working conditions and wages that are the same as those given to local workers.

The "Q" applicant must be at least eighteen years old and be able to communicate about their home country. Application is made on Form I-129.

R. Religious Workers

This category was created for religious workers coming to the U.S. to perform temporary services. The alien must have been a member of a religious organization for at least the immediately preceding two years. Three groups of religious workers can qualify: ministers of religion, professional workers in religious vocations and occupations, and other religious workers who are employed by a religious nonprofit organization, or a related tax exempt entity, under IRS definition. Religious workers can be admitted to the U.S. for an initial period of three years. The total stay is limited to five years. Aliens can apply directly at the American Consulate for the R-1 visa. They must present:

---

1. Proof that the sponsoring organization is non-profit
2. A letter from the sponsoring organization including the salary for the position; the required two years of membership in the denomination; qualifications as a minister, religious professional, or as an alien in a religious vocation; the affiliation between the religious organization in the U.S. and abroad; and the location where the alien would be working.

The spouse and minor children of religious workers are eligible for R-2 classification, which does not allow for employment.

S. Alien Informants

This classification was created for aliens who assist law enforcement agencies in supplying critical information about criminal enterprises and terrorism. It is not covered in this book.

T. NAFTA Professionals

This category is covered in Chapter 4.

NONIMMIGRANT VISA REFERENCE CHART

A-1,A-2,A-3 Ambassadors, public ministers, diplomats or consular officers assigned to represent their country in the U.S., their immediate families and servants

B-1 Temporary business visitors

B-2 Temporary visitors for pleasure

C-1 Aliens in transit through the U.S. to a third country

D Crewmen of aircraft or sea vessels

E-1 Treaty trader, spouse and minor children

E-2 Treaty investor, spouse and minor children

F-1 Students pursing academic courses of study

F-2 Spouse and minor children of F-1

G-1 thru 5 Representatives of international organizations like the United Nations and the World Bank, their family, staff and servants

H-1B Specialty occupations

H-2A Agricultural temporary workers

H-2B Non-agricultural temporary workers

H-3 Temporary trainees, special education

H-4 Spouse and minor children of H-1, H-2 and H-3 visa holders

I Representatives of foreign information media, and their family

J-1 Exchange visitors

J-2 Spouse and minor children of J-1 visa holders

K-1 Alien fiancé or fiancee of U.S. citizen and minor children

(continued on next page)

L-1	Temporary intracompany transferees
L-2	Spouse and minor children of L-1 visa holder
M-1	Students enrolled in vocational educational programs
M-2	Spouse and minor children of M-1 visa holders
N-1 thru 7	NATO visa holders
O-1, O-2, O-3	Extraordinary aliens, essential support and family
P-1, P-2, P-3	Artists, Athletes, Entertainers
Q	Cultural exchange
R-1	Religious workers
R-2	Spouse and minor children of religious workers
S-1	Informants relating to criminal enterprises
S-2	Informants related to terrorism
TN	NAFTA Professionals
TD	Dependents of NAFTA Professionals

3 VISA WAIVER PILOT PROGRAM

Two additional categories of nonimmigrant status exist in which visas are not required for admission into the U.S. The first is the Visa Waiver Pilot Program, covered in this chapter, and the second is the North American Free Trade Agreement, covered in Chapter 4.

In 1986 the INS established a Visa Waiver Pilot Program, on an experimental basis, for citizens of certain countries who wish to travel to the U.S. as visitors. It was developed to promote international tourism, and was implemented in July, 1988. The program was originally scheduled to end on September 30, 1991, but because of its success, it was extended to September 30, 1997. At the time this book went to press, Congress was considering legislation to further extend this program. In the interim, emergency measures have been put into place and ports of entry have been instructed to allow travelers to still apply for entry into the U.S. and to be admitted for a ninety day period under a visa waiver. We are confident that the Visa Waiver program will be signed into law in the near future.

Citizens of the United Kingdom were the first to be granted a benefit under this program. It has now been extended to include citizens of the following twenty five countries:

Andorra
Argentina
Australia
Austria
Belgium
Brunei
Denmark
Germany
Finland
France
Iceland
Ireland
Italy

Japan
Liechtenstein
Luxembourg
Monaco
The Netherlands
New Zealand
Norway
San Marino
Spain
Sweden
Switzerland
United Kingdom

Citizens of the countries listed above can be admitted to the U.S. for up to ninety days as B-1 or B-2 visitors. Extensions of stay or change of visa status are not permitted. Individuals who wish to participate in the program are required to complete Form I-94W, supplied by the transportation carrier, prior to inspection by a U.S. Immigration officer, and the carrier must be one that is participating in the program. The visitor must also:

---

1. Have a valid passport
2. Have a valid round trip airline ticket that has been signed by a carrier participating in the program, and be arriving on that carrier
3. Have proof of the ability to support himself or herself while in the U.S.
4. Be willing to waive any appeal rights if the immigration officer finds them inadmissible (except for asylum)
5. Be prepared to be screened by the INS upon arrival in the U.S.

Individuals taking advantage of this program are also now permitted to enter the U.S. at land border crossing points, such as Canada or Mexico.

4 The North American Free Trade Agreement (NAFTA)

In November 1993, Congress approved the North American Free Trade Agreement, commonly known as NAFTA. It became effective on January 1, 1994. NAFTA facilitates trade and investment by liberalizing the rules for entry of temporary business people among the three countries in the agreement: the United States, Mexico and Canada. While NAFTA covers many subjects, this book is concerned only with it's immigration aspects.

NAFTA affects four categories of business people, equivalent to the INS nonimmigrant categories of B-1, "E", L-1 and H-1B discussed previously. There is no limit to the number of Canadians that can enter the U.S. annually. However, no more than 5,500 citizens of Mexico can be classified as TN (Trade NAFTA) nonimmigrants each year.

1. Business Visitors

This is equivalent to our nonimmigrant B-1 category. It requires the United States, Canada and Mexico to temporarily allow a business person from another NAFTA party into the host country to engage in an occupation or profession from one of several categories of business activities: research and design; growth, manufacture and production; marketing; sales; distribution; after-sales service; and general service.

The business activity must be international in scope, and the business visitor must not be "employed" in the United States, e.g. be seeking to enter the local labor market. The primary source of compensation for the proposed business activity, as well as the actual place where profits are made, must be outside the U.S.

Applicants may apply for admission to the United States at a Port of Entry. Canadian citizens are exempt from visa requirements, but Mexican citizens must still present a valid passport with a B-1 visa, or a border crossing card. Canadian business people do not need a Form I-94, but may request one to facilitate subsequent entries into the U.S. Forms I-94 will be endorsed for "multiple entry". Mexican business people, admitted under NAFTA, will be issued a Form I-94 for a period not to exceed one year.

If an extension is needed, it may be filed with the INS on Form I-539 at least fifteen, but not more than sixty days before the expiration of stay. Derivative status for the spouse and minor unmarried children of entrants in this category does not exist, although they may be eligible to enter the U.S. as B-2 visitors.

2. Traders and Investors

This classification is similar to our E-1 and E-2 categories. It is offered to Mexican citizens for the first time. Under NAFTA, the investor category has also been broadened to include entry of Canadians and Mexicans into the U.S to: "establish, develop, administer, or provide advice or key technical services to the operation of an investment to which the business person or the business person's enterprise has committed, or is in the process of committing, a substantial amount of capital". The alien must be entering the United States in a position that is supervisory, executive or involves essential skills. Applicants for this category must obtain a visa. The American Consulates in Canada have a standard "E" visa questionnaire. The American Consulates in Mexico use an "E" visa form for Mexican citizens.

The initial approval period for an "E" visa is at least five years for Canadian citizens, and six months for Mexican citizens. The actual initial period of admission into the U.S. is one year for both Canadian and Mexican citizens. Extensions of stay can be filed on Form I-129 with the INS Regional Service Center having jurisdiction over the applicant's residence.

If a trader or investor wants to change employers, they may only do so after a written request has been approved by the INS office having jurisdiction over their residence in the U.S. After the request is granted, the applicant's Form I-94 will be endorsed on the back "employment by (name of new employer) authorized", date. Extensions may be granted in increments of not more than two years. However, when the "E" visa alien departs the U.S., he or she will only be granted a one year stay upon reentry. The spouse and minor, unmarried children of traders and investors are entitled to the same classification as the principal applicant, and are admitted into the U.S. for one year.

3. Intracompany Transferees

This category is similar to our L-1 classification for intracompany transferees. Canadian and Mexican managers, executives and people with specialized knowledge can enter the U.S. if they continue to provide services that are managerial, executive or specialized knowledge in nature. They must also be working for the same company, its affiliate or subsidiary. An L-1 petition is required of all applicants, and the applicant must establish at least one year of continuous experience abroad. See Chapter 2 for complete L-1 petition requirements.

Canadian employers can file the petition at the same time that the alien applies for admission at the U.S.-Canadian border, e.g. at Ports of Entry or PFI (pre-flight inspection stations), located in Canada. If the petition is approved, the INS inspector will give the alien a receipt for the fee collected, and send one copy of the petition to the appropriate INS Regional Service

Center for final action, and issuance of an approval notice, Form I-797. The INS inspector will then inspect the alien and issue Form I-94.

Mexican employers must file the petition with an INS Regional Service Center having jurisdiction over the alien's prospective place of employment in the U.S., and the applicant must receive an L-1 visa before being allowed to enter the U.S. The visa requirement has been waived for Canadian citizens, but not Mexican citizens.

If an extension is needed, either for Canadian or Mexican citizens, it can be made on Form I-129, with L supplement, to the appropriate INS Regional Service Center. The spouse and unmarried minor children of intracompany transferees are entitled to L-2 status. Mexican citizen spouse and children must obtain L-2 visas before they can enter the United States.

4. Professionals

This is similar to our H-1B category. NAFTA established a category for TN (Trade NAFTA) professionals. Canadians are allowed to apply for TN status at the port of entry, without any prior petition or visa approval, but Mexicans are subject to the same requirements as all professionals applying for H-1B status, including LCA and petition requirements. Self-employment in the U.S. is not permitted in TN status. TN status is available to the following listed professionals:

Accountants
Agriculturists
Agronomists
Animal breeders
Animal scientists
Apiculturists
Architects
Astronomers
Biochemists
Biologists
Chemists
College teachers
(seminary or university teachers)
Computer systems analysts
Dairy scientists
Dentists
Dietitians
Disaster relief insurance claims adjusters
Economists
Engineers
Entomologists
Epidemiologists
Foresters

Geneticists
Geologists
Geochemists
Geophysicists
Graphic designers
Horticulturists
Hotel managers
Industrial designers
Interior designers
Land surveyors
Landscape architects
Lawyers
Librarians
Management consultants
Mathematicians
(including statisticians)
Medical technologists
Meteorologists
Nutritionists
Occupational therapists
Pharmacists
Pharmacologists
Physicians (teaching or research only)
Physicists

Physiotherapists
Plant breeders
Poultry scientists
Range managers
Recreational therapists
Registered nurses
Research assistants
(for post-secondary ed. institution)
Scientific technicians

Social workers
Soil scientists
Sylviculturists
Technical publications writers
Urban planners
Vocational counselors
Veterinarians
Zoologists

The various requirements of degrees, credentials in lieu of degrees, and licenses for certain professions are confusing and beyond the scope of this book. If you believe you may be qualified under NAFTA, you should seek the advice of a qualified immigration professional.

Extensions for TN professionals are filed on Form I-129. Applications may be made at the INS Nebraska Service Center. Canadians may also apply for readmission at the border. Extensions of stay are granted for up to one year. There is no set limit on the total amount of time one may remain in the U.S. in TN status.

Spouses and unmarried minor children of TN professionals are granted TD status.

5 CHANGE OF NONIMMIGRANT STATUS AND EXTENSION OF TEMPORARY STAY

Before concluding our discussion of nonimmigrant visas, two additional types of applications need to be mentioned that apply to aliens who are currently in the U.S.: the application for change of nonimmigrant status and the extension of temporary stay.

APPLICATION FOR CHANGE OF NONIMMIGRANT STATUS

Aliens who are in the U.S. with certain types of temporary visas, and wish to change to a different visa classification, can file an application for change of nonimmigrant status. For example, an alien is in the U.S. in student (F-1) status, completes his course of study and is awarded a Master's degree in Chemical Engineering. He is then offered a temporary job as a Chemical Engineer with a U.S company. Since the alien seems to be qualified for H-1B classification, the employer could file an H-1B petition with the INS as described in Chapter 2. Another example would be that of a spouse who comes to the U.S. in L-2 status and then receives an offer of temporary professional employment. If that person is a professional under the definition of H-1B, he or she could also change status from L-2 to H-1B. The alien must file the application prior to the expiration of Form I-94, have a passport valid for the entire stay, and cannot work in the new visa status while the Application for Change of Nonimmigrant Status is pending with the INS.

The approval notice will usually be valid for the same period of time as the approved petition. The alien can remain in the U.S. as long as Form I-94 remains valid. There is no requirement that the alien travel abroad to apply for the temporary visa at an American Consulate. Applications to change status to "E", "H", "L", "O", "P" or "R" are filed on Form I-129. Applications to change status to other nonimmigrant categories are filed on Form I-539.

A change of status application cannot be filed for aliens in certain visa categories, including aliens admitted to the U.S. under the Visa Waiver Pilot Program, "C", "D", "K" and "S" aliens and certain J-1 aliens. Also an M-1 visa holder cannot change to F-1 status, nor can an M-1 student change to "H" classification, if the "M" training helped to qualify for the "H" position.

APPLICATION TO EXTEND TIME OF TEMPORARY STAY

If an alien is in the United States in B-1 or B-2 status and wants to extend his or her temporary stay, the alien can file an application with the INS on Form I-539. If a petition was originally required, as in the case of the "E", "H", "L", "O", "P" and "R", the employer must file for these extensions on Form I-129. For example, if an individual has been in the U.S. in L-1 status for three years and wishes to extend that status for an additional two years, he or she can apply to extend the status. A passport valid for the entire stay is required. The basic application consists of:

1. Form I-129-Petition for a Nonimmigrant Worker (and applicable supplement depending on temporary visa status)
2. Forms I-94 of the employee
3. Letter from the employer explaining reasons for requesting the extension
4. Form I-539 for family members and their Forms I-94
5. Applicable filing fee.

For H-1B extensions an approved labor condition application is required. If the extension is for H-2A or H-2B, a labor certification valid for the new dates must be submitted in most cases.

When the application is approved, the INS will issue a new notice of approval. The bottom half will consist of a receipt and a new Form I-94. The application must be filed prior to the expiration of Forms I-94. The alien is permitted to remain in the U.S. during the processing of the extension request, and once the application is approved, he or she can remain in the U.S. for as long as Form I-94 remains valid. Individuals in TN status may also file extension of stay requests in the U.S.

Note: aliens who are attempting to extend B-1 or B-2 status must provide the INS with a reasonable explanation as to why they were unable to complete their visit within the time period originally authorized. The alien must also prove that he or she is really still a visitor. It is always a good idea to file a copy of a return trip airline ticket with the application as proof that the stay is, indeed, temporary.

Individuals who are in the U.S. in "C", "D", "K" or "S" status, and those who have entered the U.S. in B-1 or B-2 status under the Visa Waiver Pilot Program described earlier, are not eligible for extensions of temporary stay.

IMMIGRANT VISAS

The terms "immigrant visa", "permanent resident", "resident alien" and "green card" status all imply the same thing. They represent the right of a foreign national to permanently live and work in the United States. This chapter explains how the U.S. Government uses quotas and a preference system to allocate immigrant visas. Some exceptions, such as the concept of "cross-chargeability" are also discussed. Each of the immigrant visa categories is then explained, including procedures for applying, and the documents required to do so.

If you do not qualify for one of the nonimmigrant categories described in earlier chapters, you may only be able to apply under an immigrant category. The procedure for obtaining an immigrant visa is a lengthy one and can be extremely confusing and frustrating to applicants. One reason for the frustration stems from the inability to predict the actual time it will take to complete the application process.

Timing depends on a variety of factors, such as following the correct filing procedures for each type of application, the extent of processing backlogs in the government offices, which varies from state to state, and the availability of the quota. In some cases, the procedure can be completed in as little as a few months while in other circumstances, applicants from certain countries can wait for ten years or longer! Why is there such a variation in timing for immigrant visa processing?

THE QUOTA

The United States Congress established a very complicated system for issuing immigrant visas. Each month the Department of State in Washington, DC prints a visa bulletin, which lists the availability of visas for every country for that particular month. Only a limited number of immigrant visas are generally issued each year. This limitation is called the "quota" and is based on an alien's country of birth. A sample visa bulletin is supplied at the end of this chapter.

An individual born in India is eligible for one of the visas allocated to that country. If that same Indian citizen has become a citizen of another country, for example Canada, he or she is still subject to the Indian quota. This is because our quota system is based on the alien's country of birth, not the country of citizenship. The country quota under which an applicant must apply for an immigrant visa is commonly referred to as the alien's "chargeability". There are four exceptions to chargeability by place of birth. These exceptions are known as "cross-chargeability".

1. If the alien is married to another alien who is a citizen of a different country, the couple can apply under the more favorable quota. For example, if a woman born in the Philippines is married to a man born in Canada, the application for permanent residence can be made under either the Philippine or Canadian quota. In this case, the Canadian quota would be more favorable than that for the Philippines.

2. If the alien was accidentally born in a different country from the place of birth of his or her parents, and the parents were not firmly settled in the country where the child was born, the alien can be charged to the place of birth of either parent. For example, a Venezuelan couple on vacation in Mexico give birth to a baby. Subsequently, the family immigrates to the U.S. The baby will be charged to the Venezuelan rather than the Mexican quota.

If the parents never immigrated to the U.S., but this child later immigrated as an adult, he or she could still be charged to the Venezuelan quota, as long as proof existed that the child's place of birth was, indeed, an accident.

3. Minor children can be charged to either parent's place of birth. For example, a Canadian executive of an international company is sent to work in Taiwan for two years. His British born wife accompanies him. During the couple's stay in Taiwan, the wife gives birth to a child. At the end of the two years, the family is transferred to the U.S. in L-1 status. They subsequently apply for permanent residence. The Taiwan born child could be charged either to the Canadian or British quota.

4. Former U.S. citizens can be charged to their country of last residence or country of citizenship.

Why are these cross-chargeability categories important? Because several countries have many more than their maximum allowable number of citizens applying for permanent residence in the U.S. each year. This results in long delays in obtaining green cards. When an applicant benefits from cross-chargeability, the processing time can be significantly shortened.

THE PREFERENCE SYSTEM

Immigrant visas are currently grouped into two general categories:

1) Family sponsored preferences
2) Employment based preferences.

This is known as the preference system.

Family Based Preferences

The preference categories assigned to relatives of U.S. citizens or permanent residents, and the number of visas issued annually in each category are as follows:

- ◆ <u>Family first preference</u>: Unmarried sons and daughters (over 21 years of age) of U.S. citizens: 23,400 plus any numbers not used in fourth preference.

- ◆ <u>Family second preference</u>: Spouses, children and unmarried sons and daughters of permanent residents: 114,200 plus the number by which the worldwide family preference allocation exceeds 226,000, and any numbers not used in first preference.

  Family 2A- Spouses and children (unmarried, under 21) are granted 77% of the second preference numbers, and 75% of these are exempt from the "per country limitation".

  Family 2B-Adult unmarried sons and daughters of permanent residents are entitled to the remaining 23% of the second preference allocation.

- ◆ <u>Family third preference</u>: married sons and daughters of U.S. citizens: 23,400 plus any numbers not used in first and second preference.

- ◆ <u>Family fourth preference</u>: brothers and sisters of adult U.S. citizens: 65,000 plus any numbers not used in family first, second or third preference

In each category defined above, the U.S. citizen or permanent resident files a petition with the INS. It consists of:

---

1. Form I-130- Petition for Alien Relative
2. Documentary proof that the petitioner is a U.S. citizen or permanent resident
3. Documentary proof that the petitioner and the alien are related
4. Applicable filing fee.

Note: Second preference spouse cases also require separate photos of petitioner and beneficiary and biographic data forms.

When the INS receives the petition, it is date stamped. This date becomes the alien's "priority date" on the waiting list for permanent residence.

As soon as the INS approves the petition, it forwards the approval notice to the petitioner and to the American Consulate where the alien will apply for the immigrant visa, if the beneficiary is not in the U.S. The Consulate then sends an information packet to the applicant, which he or she completes and returns. When the priority date is reached, the alien receives a notice to appear at the Consulate, with accompanying family members, for a final interview. He or she also receives detailed instructions about the documents that the applicants will be required to present at the interview, including directions for completing medical examinations.

If the immigrant visa application is approved at the interview, the alien is given a sealed envelope, which he or she then takes to the U.S. The first entry into the U.S. must be made within four months of the final interview. The Immigration Officer at the point of entry into the U.S. takes the envelope and stamps a permanent resident visa in the passport. The INS then forwards certain documents to the Immigration Card Facility in Texas for processing. The resident alien is free to travel in and out of the U.S. as long as the stamp in the passport is valid. The final green card is mailed from Texas to the applicant's new address in the U.S. This usually takes ninety days. If the card is not received within that time period, a written follow-up should be made to the Immigration Card Facility on Form G-731 to determine why the card has not been received.

If the beneficiary is in the U.S., it may be possible to complete the application process in the U.S. When the priority date is reached, the alien files an Application for Adjustment of Status at the immigration office having jurisdiction over the applicant's place of residence.

If the applicant is in the United States in legal immigration status, has not accepted unauthorized employment, and has never violated his or her status, the applicant can apply with the following documents:

1. I-130 approval notice
2. Form I-485-Application to Register Permanent Resident or Adjust Status
3. Form G-325A -Biographic Information- for each family member over the age of fourteen
4. Photographs for each family member that must meet exact specifications provided by the INS
5. Completed fingerprint charts for each applicant over the age of fourteen and under the age of seventy five
6. Copy of Form I-94 for each applicant
7. Copy of any evidence showing continuous lawful status
8. Copy of passport
9. IRS Form 9003
10. Affidavit of support or employment letter
11. The applicable filing fee for each I-485 being submitted
12. Medical examination report (required at time of application in some INS offices, but not all).

The beneficiary must also submit an Affidavit of Support for the family and provide birth and marriage certificates, and proof of termination of previous marriages, if applicable. The INS requires that birth certificates be "long form", showing names of parents. All personal documents must be accompanied by certified English translations. In some jurisdictions, the INS office routinely requests other documents that are not listed above.

The following groups of aliens have also been able adjust status under a law that expired on September 30, 1997. This immigration law is known as Section 245(i). Although Congress is not renewing this law, they have indicated that aliens who are the beneficiaries of visa petitions and labor certification applications filed by January 14, 1998 will be "grandfathered". This means that that the following groups of aliens will be allowed to continue to adjust status under Section 245(i).

1. Aliens who entered the U.S. illegally
2. Aliens who have remained in the U.S. beyond their authorized stay
3. Aliens who have accepted unauthorized employment.

Note: Congress has also decided to permit certain employment-based visa applicants to adjust status if they are currently maintaining lawful status and have not previously been out out status for more than an aggregate of 180 days. This provision is distinct from the grandfathering provision. (When this book went to print, the above had not yet been signed into law, and is subject to change.)

Applicants under the three categories shown above need to submit all documents shown in the previous box. In addition, a Form I-485A supplement must be filed along with a $1000.00 penalty fee for each applicant. This fee is waived for the following categories of applicants:

1. Children under age seventeen
2. An alien who is the spouse or unmarried child of an individual who was legalized under the Immigration Reform and Control Act of 1986 and who was: a) The spouse or unmarried child of the legalized alien as of May 5, 1988; b) Entered the United States before May 5, 1988 and re sided here on that date; c) Applied for family unity benefits under the Immigration Act of 1990.

Although the application forms that need to be filed with the INS may differ somewhat from office to office, the events leading up to the final interview are essentially the same as attending a final interview at an American

Consulate. At the final interview the applicants must present the following:

> 1. Valid passports
> 2. Medical reports (instructions for examination provided by the INS)
> 3. Original birth certificates, marriage certificate and proof of the termination of prior marriages, if applicable
> 4. Current letter of employment
> 5. Affidavit of support for the accompanying family members.

The applicant's passport, and those of accompanying family members, will be stamped with the temporary green card upon approval of the case. The INS will then forward the required documents to the Immigration Card Facility in Texas for processing of the green cards.

Applicants who are eligible to complete their immigrant visa applications in the United States but choose not to, may complete their applications at an American Consulate abroad. However, these applicants will be required to remain outside the United States for ninety days. See previous discussion on applying for an immigrant visa at an American Consulate.

Applicants With Permanent Offers of Employment

The Immigration Act of 1990 allows for 140,000 immigrant visas to be issued each year for employment based petitions. The preference categories assigned to applicants who have permanent offers of employment in the U.S., and the number of visas issued in each category are as follows:

◆ Employment Based First Preference: Priority Workers: 40,000 plus those numbers not used for fourth and fifth preference. Priority workers include aliens of extraordinary ability in the arts, sciences, business, education and athletics; managers and executives of international companies being transferred permanently to the U.S.; and outstanding professors and researchers. Labor certification is not required for employment based first preference (see explanation in Chapter 7). Please note that priority workers of "extraordinary ability" do not require an offer of employment as long as they will continue to work in their area of expertise. This only applies to extraordinary ability.

◆ Employment Based Second Preference: Members of the professions holding advanced degrees (any degree above a bachelors) and people of exceptional merit and ability in the sciences, arts or business: 40,000 plus those numbers not used in first preference. Labor certification is required.

◆   Employment Based Third Preference: Skilled workers
(must be filling a position that requires two years of training
and experience), professionals with bachelors degrees
and unskilled workers: 40,000 plus those numbers not used in
first and second preference. Labor certification is required.
Please note that only 10,000 of the 40,000 visas in this category
will be allocated to unskilled workers.

◆   Employment Based Fourth Preference: Certain "special"
immigrants: 10,000. This category includes juveniles under
court protection; employees of the American Consulate in Hong
Kong; and religious workers, such as ministers, who have at
least a bachelor's degree. Please note that not more than 5,000 of
these visas will be issued to religious workers. (Application to be
filed on Form I-360).

◆   Employment Based Fifth Preference: Employment creation
(investors): 10,000, with not less than 3000 reserved for investors
who invest in a targeted rural or high-unemployment area in the
U.S. There is no labor certification requirement in this category,
however there are other strict criteria, which must be met such
as the dollar amount of the investment and the number of jobs the
investment will create for U.S. workers. See Chapter 8.

Before an application for permanent residence can be made based on an offer of employment in the employment based second and third preference
categories, a basis of eligibility for filing the petition must be established.
This usually requires that the sponsoring employer file an Application for
Alien Employment Certification with the U.S. Department of Labor. This
application should eventually result in the issuance of a Labor Certification. Other aliens may establish a basis of eligibility under a category called
"Schedule A", and still others, under another employment based category.
In these cases, the U.S. Department of Labor has determined that it is not
necessary for a sponsoring employer to obtain Labor Certification. The Labor Certification process, Schedule A, and other employment based categories are discussed in Chapter 7.

Once the alien has established a basis for eligibility, and a visa number becomes available based on the priority date, the procedure for completing the
application is similar to the procedure for relatives of U.S. citizens or permanent residents discussed earlier in this chapter.

INDIVIDUALS NOT SUBJECT TO QUOTA LIMITATIONS

Two common categories of individuals who are not subject to the numerical limitations of the quota described above are:

1) Applicants who are Immediate Relatives of U.S. Citizens: Citizenship may be on the basis of birth in the U.S. or through naturalization. Immediate relatives includes spouses, unmarried sons and daughters under the age of twenty one, and parents of adult citizens (over the age of 21). This category also includes spouses of deceased U.S. citizens, in certain cases. (This last application is made on Form I-360-Petition for Amerasian, Widow or Special Immigrant.)

Although the quota system does not apply, the sponsor is still required to file an I-130 petition with the INS before the relative can immigrate to America. If the relative is in the U.S. in legal status, the entire application process can be completed within a few months. If the relative applies at an American Consulate overseas, the processing time will vary according to the administrative backlogs at the INS and at the Consulate abroad.

In the case of husbands or wives, an applicant who has been married for less than two years will be granted a conditional green card. After two years, the applicant will be required to file another application with the INS on Form I-751 (Petition to Remove the Conditions of Residence). The couple will be required to prove that they entered into the marriage in good faith and are still married to each other. At that point, the conditional status will be removed and the applicant will be issued a permanent green card.

Note: There are waivers available for battered spouses and in cases of divorce. You should seek the advice of a professional if you fall into either of these categories.

2) Refugees: Refugees are those who are unwilling to, or cannot, return to their country of origin because they fear persecution based on race, religion, nationality, political views or membership in a particular group. Each year the President of the United States, together with Congress, decides on the number of applicants who will be admitted to the U.S. as refugees or asylees. The refugee application processes are complex and are not covered in this book.

United States Department of State
Bureau of Consular Affairs

VISA BULLETIN

Number 78   Volume VII   **Washington, D.C.**

IMMIGRANT NUMBERS FOR SEPTEMBER 1997

A. STATUTORY NUMBERS

1. This bulletin summarizes the availability of immigrant numbers during September. Consular officers are required to report to the Department of State documentarily qualified applicants for numerically limited visas; the Immigration and Naturalization Service reports applicants for adjustment of status. Allocations were made, to the extent possible under the numerical limitations, for the demand received by July 8th in the chronological order of the reported priority dates.
If the demand could not be satisfied within the statutory or regulatory limits, the category or foreign state in which demand was excessive was deemed oversubscribed. The cut-off date for an oversubscribed category is the priority date of the first applicant who could not be reached within the numerical limits. Only applicants who have a priority date earlier than the cut-off date may be allotted a number. Immediately that it becomes necessary during the monthly allocation process to retrogress a cut-off date, supplemental requests for numbers will be honored only if the priority date falls within the new cut-off date.

2. The fiscal year 1997 limit for family-sponsored preference immigrants determined in accordance with Section 201 of the Immigration and Nationality Act (INA) is 226,000. The fiscal year 1997 limit for employment-based preference immigrants calculated under INA 201 is 140,000. Section 202 prescribes that the per-country limit for preference immigrants is set at 7% of the total annual family-sponsored and employment-based preference limits, i.e., 25,620 for FY-1997. The dependent area limit is set at 2%, or 7,320.

3. Section 203 of the INA prescribes preference classes for allotment of immigrant visas as follows:

FAMILY-SPONSORED PREFERENCES

First: Unmarried Sons and Daughters of Citizens: 23,400 plus any numbers not required for fourth preference.

Second: Spouses and Children, and Unmarried Sons and Daughters of Permanent Residents: 114,200, plus the number (if any) by which the worldwide family preference level exceeds 226,000, and any unused first preference numbers:

A. Spouses and Children: 77% of the overall second preference limitation, of which 75% are exempt from the per-country limit;

B. Unmarried Sons and Daughters (21 years of age or older): 23% of the overall second preference limitation.

Third: Married Sons and Daughters of Citizens: 23,400, plus any numbers not required by first and second preferences.

Fourth: Brothers and Sisters of Adult Citizens: 65,000, plus any numbers not required by first three preferences. 55

EMPLOYMENT-BASED PREFERENCES

First: Priority Workers: 28.6% of the worldwide employment-based preference level, plus any numbers not required for fourth and fifth preferences.

Second: Members of the Professions Holding Advanced Degrees or Persons of Exceptional Ability: 28.6% of the worldwide employment-based preference level, plus any numbers not required by first preference.

Third: Skilled Workers, Professionals, and Other Workers: 28.6% of the worldwide level, plus any numbers not required by first and second preferences, not more than 10,000 of which to "Other Workers".

Fourth: Certain Special Immigrants: 7.1% of the worldwide level.

Fifth: Employment Creation: 7.1% of the worldwide level, not less than 3,000 of which reserved for investors in a targeted rural or high-unemployment area, and 300 set aside for investors in regional centers by Sec. 610 of P.L. 102-395.

4.   INA Section 203(e) provides that family-sponsored and employment-based preference visas be issued to eligible immigrants in the order in which a petition in behalf of each has been filed. Section 203(d) provides that spouses and children of preference immigrants are entitled to the same status, and the same order of consideration, if accompanying or following to join the principal. The visa prorating provisions of Section 202(e) apply to allocations for a foreign state or dependent area when visa demand exceeds the per-country limit. These provisions apply at present to the following oversubscribed chargeability areas: INDIA, MEXICO, and PHILIPPINES.

5.   On the chart below, the listing of a date for any class indicates that the class is oversubscribed (see paragraph 1); "C" means current, i.e., numbers are available for all qualified applicants; and "U" means unavailable, i.e., no numbers are available. (NOTE: Numbers are available only for applicants whose priority date is earlier than the cut-off date listed below.)

PREFERENCES

	All Charge-ability Areas Except Those Listed	INDIA	MEXICO	PHILIPPINES
Family				
1st	15FEB94	15FEB94	15FEB94	15SEP86
2A*	15MAY93	15MAY93	22AUG92	15MAY93
2B	08MAY91	08MAY91	01MAY91	08MAY91
3rd	01APR94	01APR94	08NOV88	01APR86
4th	01FEB87	01MAY85	08AUG86	01MAR78

*NOTE: For September, 2A numbers EXEMPT from per-country limit are available to applicants from all countries with priority dates earlier than 22AUG92. 2A numbers SUBJECT to per-country limit are available to applicants chargeable to all countries EXCEPT MEXICO with priority dates beginning 22AUG92 and earlier than 15MAY93. (2A numbers subject to per-country limit are "unavailable" for applicants chargeable to MEXICO.)

September 1997

	All Charge- ability Areas Except Those Listed	INDIA	MEXICO	PHILIPPINES
Employment- Based				
1st	C	C	*C	C
2nd	C	C	C	C
3rd	C	08DEC95	C	C
Other Workers	01JUL88	01JUL88	01JUL88	01JUL88
4th	C	C	C	C
Certain Religious Workers	01FEB95	01FEB95	01FEB95	01FEB95
5th	C	C	C	C
Targeted Employ- ment Areas/ Regional Centers	C	C	C	C

The Department of State has available a recorded message with visa availability information which can be heard at: (area code 202) 663-1541. This recording will be updated in the middle of each month with information on cut-off dates for the following month.

B.   DIVERSITY IMMIGRANT (DV) CATEGORY

Section 203(c) of the Immigration and Nationality Act provides 55,000 immigrant visas each fiscal year to provide immigration opportunities for persons from countries other than the principal sources of current immigration to the United States. DV visas are divided among six geographic regions. Not more than 3,850 visas (7% of the 55,000 visa limit) may be provided to immigrants from any one country.

This page intentionally left blank

Use for notes

7 LABOR CERTIFICATION, SCHEDULE A AND OTHER EXEMPTIONS

As explained in Chapter 6, aliens who are offered permanent employment in the U.S. must establish a basis of eligibility for filing an employment based preference petition, either through labor certification (employment based preference Category 2 and 3), exemption from labor certification (employment based Categories 1, 4 and 5) or under a Schedule A category.

This chapter describes the various stages involved in obtaining general labor certification for employment based preference Categories 2 and 3, and exemptions from labor certification. It should be noted that the Department of Labor will not approve labor certifications for certain unskilled jobs.

THE LABOR CERTIFICATION PROCESS

Aliens who have been offered permanent employment in the U.S., and who do not meet the criteria for exemption from labor certification, must obtain Alien Employment Certification, commonly referred to as labor certification from the U.S. Department of Labor (DOL). The DOL must be satisfied that there are no qualified U.S. workers available to fill the permanent job offered to the alien, and that the working conditions and wages offered for the position will not have an adverse effect on the U.S. labor market. Once the labor certification is approved, it serves as the basis for filing an employment based 2nd or 3rd preference petition with the INS. (Appendix C contains Regional Department of Labor office addresses, and the jurisdictions that they cover.)

To obtain labor certification, the employer must demonstrate that he or she has followed a precise program of recruitment that tests the local labor market for qualified and available U.S. workers in the geographic area where the job will be filled. The steps in this process are as follows:

✔ **Step 1**: The employer files completed (in duplicate) Forms ETA 750A (Offer of Employment) & ETA 750B (Statement of Qualifications of Alien) with the State office of the DOL where the job will be filled. The Offer of Employment is completed and signed by the employer and the Statement of Qualifications of Alien is completed and signed by the alien.

✔ **Step 2**: The DOL date stamps the application upon receipt, and this becomes the alien's priority date for quota purposes. The application is then reviewed by the DOL; in some cases, it may be returned to the employer for additional information or clarification of certain job requirements.

✔ **Step 3:** Once the inquiries are satisfied, or if no clarification is required, the DOL forwards the application to the State Employment Service Office. This office opens a thirty day job order and issues recruitment instructions to the employer. The timing between Steps 1 and 3 varies considerably from one State Employment Service Office to another. In states where the DOL processes very few applications, the timing may be quite short. In other states, such as New York, where the DOL receives thousands of applications, the employer may not receive any correspondence for close to a year!

✔ **Step 4**: The employer must follow the recruitment instructions provided by the DOL. The standard procedure is that the employer places an advertisement in a newspaper of general circulation, one that is most likely to bring responses, for at least three consecutive days, posts the job opening in the company for ten consecutive business days, and/or sends a notice of the application to its employees' bargaining representative, if one exists. The employer is responsible for paying for these ads.

The advertisement and posting must include the job title, position description, academic qualifications, experience and any other special requirements, as well as the salary offered. The name of the employer does not appear in the advertisement. Instead, the DOL assigns it a code number (job order number) which must appear in the ad; applicants must be instructed in the ad to apply directly to the Department of Labor. The job posting gives any qualified U.S. worker in the company the opportunity to apply for the job. Many employers hesitate to run ads and post jobs internally with salary figures. Even though this may not be the normal employer practice, for purposes of obtaining labor certification it is virtually essential.

✔ **Step 5**: After the ad appears and the posting is completed, the employer must send the newspaper ads and the posting to the DOL.

If the DOL receives any responses to the ads, it review the resumes, copies and records the responses, and forwards the qualified resumes to the employer. The employer must conduct an interview with all respondents, and keep detailed records as to why the applicant did not qualify for the position. If an applicant cannot be disqualified, the Department of Labor will refuse to certify the position. The same process applies to respondents to the internal posting.

✔ **Step 6**: At the end of the thirty day period, the employer must submit the results of recruitment to the DOL, with copies of the resumes received. The recruitment results must list the number of applicants, their names, (and in some jurisdictions addresses and telephone numbers) and why they were not qualified for the position. The State Office of the DOL then forwards the application to the Certifying Officer at the Regional Office of the U.S. Department of Labor.

✔ **Step 7**: The Regional Certifying Officer reviews the application and issues either a Notice of Approval of Application for Alien Employment Certification or a Notice of Findings. A Notice of Findings is not a denial, but rather a formal request for additional information, documentation or clarification. The employer is given a thirty five day period of time to respond to the notice in writing. If the Labor Department is satisfied with the response, a Notice of Approval will be issued. If the application is denied, an appeal process is available.

The total processing time for labor certification is six months to one year in less busy jurisdictions and up to two years in states that process large volumes of cases. Once the application is approved, a second or third employment based preference petition can be filed with the INS as follows:

---

1. Form I-140- Immigrant Petition for Alien Worker
2. Original approved Labor Certification
3. Proof that the alien possesses all the qualifications stated in the labor certification (education, experience, etc.)
4. The applicable filing fee.

In some cases, especially where the petitioning employer is unknown to the INS, the employer must also submit proof of its ability to pay the wages stated in the labor certification application. This can be in the form of the company's federal tax return, an annual report, or an audited financial statement.

When the I-140 petition is approved, a similar procedure is followed to complete the application for permanent residence as in relative (I-130) cases - e.g. by filing an Application for Adjustment of Status with the INS as described above. The final interview will be scheduled at the INS and the alien will usually be able to complete his or her case in the U.S. within several months.

Note: Previously, I-140 petitions and applications for adjustment of status could be filed simultaneously, in cases where, for example, an alien had an approved labor certification, with a current priority date. This is no longer the case.

SCHEDULE A CATEGORIES

In some cases, known as Schedule A, the U.S. Department of Labor has determined that the sponsoring employer need not obtain labor certification. There are presently two Schedule A categories:

◆ Schedule A Group I: Applies to professional nurses and physical therapists. In each case, the alien must have very specific credentials, including licenses, and must have passed certain exams required by each state to practice their vocation in the United States. Labor certifications are not available to professional nurses and physical therapists, even if their Schedule A Group I applications are denied.

◆ Schedule A Group II: Applies to aliens who have exceptional ability in the arts and sciences and may not qualify under employment based first preference. This category is primarily reserved for individuals who have received widespread international acclaim in their specific field, such as scientists, professors, and authors. The INS has very stringent documentary requirements for Schedule A Group II classification, including testimonial letters from experts in the alien's field of endeavor, published works by or about the alien, invitations extended to the alien to speak at international conferences, and awards.

Schedule A applications are filed directly with the INS Regional Service Center. Once the application is approved, and the priority date becomes current, the permanent residence application can be completed through adjustment of status, or by visa processing at an American Consulate. The procedures are the same as for aliens who have approved labor certifications, described above.

NATIONAL INTEREST WAIVER

An alien may seek a waiver of the offer of employment by establishing that his admission to permanent residence would be in the "national interest". There is no hard and fast rule nor any statutory standards as to what will qualify an alien for a National Interest Waiver. The INS considers each case on an individual basis. The procedure is to file Form I-140 together with evidence to establish that the alien's admission to the United States for permanent residence would be in the national interest. Factors that have been considered in successful cases include:

• The alien's admission will improve the U.S. economy.

• The alien's admission will improve wages and working conditions of U.S. workers.

• The alien's admission will improve educational and training programs for U.S. children and underqualified workers.

• The alien's admission will provide more affordable housing for young, aged, or poor U.S. residents.

• The alien's admission will improve the U.S. environment and lead to more productive use of the national resources.

* The alien's admission is requested by an interested U.S. government agency.

Many of the cases in which national interest waivers have been approved were supported by affidavits from well-known, established and influential people or organizations. For example, an application being submitted for a scientist should contain affidavits from leading scientists, representatives of scientific institutions, and from other organizations associated with the type of research to be pursued. Documenting past achievements, as well as proof that the alien has already created jobs, turned around a business or created an increase in exports or other economic improvements should prove instrumental in gaining approval.

OTHER EMPLOYMENT BASED CATEGORIES

Aliens applying for permanent residence in employment based preference Categories 1, 4 and 5 do not require labor certification. Aliens in employment based preference categories 2 & 3, who can establish that their admission is in the "National Interest", also do not require labor certification. Application is made directly to the INS on Form I-140- Immigrant Petition for Ali   Worker in employment based preference Categories 1, 2 & 3, on Form I-5   merasian, Widow or Special Immigrant in employment ba   on Form I-526- Immigrant Petition by A   d preference Category 5. Support-
i   the category in which the alien is
a

This page intentionally left blank

Use for Notes

8 Immigrant Visas for Alien Investors

The Immigration Act of 1990 created a new preference category for immigrants who are able to invest at least $1 million in the United States.

Immigrant visas are available, subject to quota limitations (approximately 10,000 annually), for immigrants seeking to enter the United States to engage in a new commercial enterprise. This new business must benefit the U.S. economy and create at least ten full-time jobs for U.S. citizens or permanent residents, other than the applicant or his or her immediate family.

The minimum amount of the investment is $1 million, although the INS may consider less if the investment is in a "targeted employment" area, i.e., one where the unemployment rate is 150% of the national average. The investment must have been made after November 29, 1990.

Under this category, the term "investment" generally means that the alien must place his or her capital at risk for the purpose of generating a profit. The company must have been formed for the "ongoing conduct of lawful business". The investment must be in a commercial enterprise that generates active income. Apartment buildings, for example, would not qualify, since the income they generate is considered passive. The term "capital" is defined as "cash, equipment, inventory, tangible property, cash equivalents and indebtedness secured by the investor's assets, provided he or she is personally liable".

The enterprise may be a sole proprietorship, a partnership, a holding company, a joint venture, a corporation or other entity publicly or privately owned. The investment does not have to be completed, but the investor must be "in the process" of investing, showing an actual commitment of funds.

Generally, the investment must be in either:

1) A newly created business
2) The purchase of an existing business and simultaneous or subsequent restructuring or reorganization such that a new commercial enterprise results
3) The expansion of an existing business so long as there is a substantial change of at least 140% in either net worth or in the number of employees of the company.

Debt can be used to secure capital, provided that the alien is personally and primarily liable, and the debt is not secured against the assets of the enterprise. Capital may come from abroad, but ownership of the capital must be established.

The investor will also have to show that he will be actively engaged in the management of the enterprise. Any assets or capital derived from illegal means or criminal activity will not be considered.

Generally, the documents for the immigrant investor are those that would establish the investment, that is, proof of the capital invested, proof of the creation of new jobs, proof of the alien's management position and evidence of the nature of the enterprise. Form I-526- Immigrant Petition by Alien Entrepreneur, is also required.

The legal definitions and rules for alien investors are complex, and you should seek the advice of a professional if you intend to pursue this category.

9 THE ANNUAL VISA LOTTERY PROGRAM

In 1995, the Immigration and Nationality Act established an annual visa lottery. Natives of certain countries, selected by a mathematical formula, are able to compete for visas in this category. The numerical limit on these types of visas is 55,000 per year. The applicant can apply either from within the U.S. or from outside the U.S.

In 1995 the program was known as the DV-1 lottery. In subsequent years the identifying symbol will be "DV" followed by the fiscal year. For example, the 1999 lottery is known as DV-99. (The government fiscal year begins on October 1 and ends on September 30.) the registration period for DV-99 will start October 24, 1997 and end on November 24, 1997.

Applications must be typed or clearly printed. They are mailed to one of six addresses, depending upon the region of the applicant's native country. For the DV-99 lottery the addresses were as follows:

ASIA:

DV-99 Program
National Visa Center
Portsmouth, NH 00210
USA

**SOUTH AMERICA,
CENTRAL AMERICA
CARIBBEAN:**

DV-99 Program
National Visa Center
Portsmouth, NH 00211
USA

EUROPE:

DV-99 Program
National Visa Center
Portsmouth, NH 00212
USA

AFRICA:

DV-99 Program
National Visa Center
Portsmouth, NH 00213
USA

OCEANIA:

DV-99 Program
National Visa Center
Portsmouth, NH 00214
USA

**NORTH AMERICA:
(Bahamas only)**

DV-99 Program
National Visa Center
Portsmouth, NH 00215
USA

Only one application per person may be submitted. Multiple applications disqualify an applicant from registration. Applications are selected in random order from all applications received during the eligibility period. In other words, the last application submitted has just as good a chance of selection as the first one submitted. Applications are to be sent by regular mail or air mail only. Any other form of delivery invalidates the application.

There is no application form or fee required. Each application must, however, contain the following information:

✔ Applicant's full name, with last name, first name and middle name (in that order). The last name should be underlined.

✔ Applicant's date and place of birth with day, month and year of birth (in that order) and place of birth with city/town, district/county/province, and country (in that order). Use current name of country.

✔ Applicant's native country if different than country of birth. Native means someone born within one of the qualifying countries and someone entitled to be charged to such country under the Immigration laws. (See Chapter 6 for explanation of chargeability.)

✔ Name, date and place of birth of applicant's spouse and children, if any.

✔ Applicant's mailing address (and phone number if possible).

✔ Recent photograph 1 1/2 inches square (37 mm.) with applicants name printed across the back. The photograph must be taped to the application.

✔ Signature of principal applicant.

Special requirements for the DV lottery are as follows:

1. Each applicant must have a high school education or its equivalent
or
2. Within the past five years, have had two years of work experience in an occupation requiring at least two years of training or experience.

After the end of the application period, a computer will randomly select cases from among all the applicants from each geographic region. All applications received during the mail-in period will have an equal chance of being selected, so there is no advantage to mailing an application early. The applications selected will be "registered" and assigned a case number that will reflect their lottery rank order.

If you are selected, you will receive a letter from the National Visa Center with your name, lottery rank order and country of chargeability, as well as instructions on how to complete the process. Once you get this letter it is imperative that you complete all applications, follow the instructions and file the necessary documents **immediately**. This is because not all the people selected will be able to complete their cases. Approximately 100,000 applications will initially be chosen, but only 55,000 visas are available. Successful applicants may either apply for an immigrant visa at the American Consulate in their country of residence or, if they are in the United States and are eligible to adjust status, apply at the INS office having jurisdiction over their place of residence.

The formal visa application made at the American Consulate consists of:

1. Optional Form- 230 I & II- Special Lottery Form
2. Police Certificates where applicable
3. Birth certificates
4. Marriage certificate or proof of termination of prior marriages
5. Proof of high school education or equivalent, or required work experience
6. Photographs
7. Completed medical examination
8. Proof of support or job offer for permanent employment.

The application for adjustment of status filed at the INS is similar to the application for adjustment of status described in Chapter 6. In addition, the applicant must provide:

1. Copy of the notification letter from the National Visa Center
2. Proof of high school education or equivalent, or required work experience
3. Proof of support or job offer

Applicants who are not selected <u>will not</u> be notified. All notification letters are expected to be sent between April and July 1998. If you do not receive a letter within this time frame, you have not been selected.

Countries that qualify for DV-99 are as follows:

Africa
Algeria, Angola, Benin, Botswana, Burkina, Burundi, Cameroon, Cape Verde, Central African Republic, Chad, Comoros, Congo, Coe D'Ivoire, Djibouti, Egypt, Equatorial Guinea, Eritrea, Ethiopia, Gabon, The Gambia, Ghana, Guinea, Guinea-Bissau, Kenya, Lesotho, Liberia, Libya, Madagascar, Malawi, Mali, Mauritania, Mauritius, Morocco, Mozambique, Namibia, Niger, Nigeria, Rwanda, Sao Tome and Principe, Senegal, Sey-

chelles, Sierra Leone, Somalia, South Africa, Sudan, Swaziland, Tanzania, Togo, Tunisia, Uganda, Zaire, Zambia, Zimbabwe.

Asia
Afghanistan, Bahrain, Bangladesh, Bhutan, Brunei, Burma, Cambodia, Hong Kong, Indonesia, Iran, Iraq, Israel, Japan, Jordan, North Korea, Kuwait, Laos, Lebanon, Malaysia, Maldives, Mongolia, Nepal, Oman, Pakistan, Qatar, Saudi Arabia, Singapore, Sri Lanka, Syria, Thailand, United Arab Emirates, Yemen.

Europe
Albania, Andorra, Armenia Austria, Azerbaijan, Belarus, Belgium, Bosnia and Herzegovina, Bulgaria, Croatia, Cyprus, Czech Republic, Denmark, Estonia, Finland, France, Georgia, Germany, Greece, Hungary, Iceland, Ireland, Italy, Kazakhstan, Kyrgyzstan, Latvia, Liechtenstein, Lithuania, Luxembourg, Macedonia, Malta, Moldova, Monaco, Montenegro, Netherlands, Northern Ireland, Norway, Portugal, Romania, Russia, San Marino, Serbia, Slovakia, Slovenia, Spain, Sweden, Switzerland, Tajikistan, Turkey, Turkmenistan, Ukraine, Uzbekistan, Vatican City.

North America
The Bahamas

Oceania

Australia, Fiji, Kiribati, Marshall Islands, Micronesia, Nauru, New Zealand, Palau, Papua New Guinea, Solomon Islands, Tonga, Tuvalu, Vanuatu, Western Samoa.

South America, Central America and the Caribbean

Antigua and Barbuda, Argentina, Barbados, Belize, Bolivia, Brazil, Chile, Costa Rica, Cuba, Dominica, Ecuador, Grenada, Guatemala, Guyana, Haiti, Honduras, Nicaragua, Panama, Paraguay, Peru, Saint Kitts and Nevis, Saint Lucia, Saint Vincent and the Grenadines, Suriname, Trinidad and Tobago, Uruguay, Venezuela.

Note: People in the U.S. who would like information about this program can call the Department of State's Visa Lottery Information Center at 1-900-884-8840.

10 NATURALIZATION

Aliens elect to become citizens of the United States in order to reap the benefits, such as the right to vote, the right to obtain a U.S. passport, and the ability to sponsor relatives for permanent residence. This chapter describes the rules and procedures for applying for citizenship or naturalization.

Permanent residents are eligible for naturalization five years after permanent residence is granted. The applicant must have physically resided in the U.S. for at least two and one half years out of the five years and have been a resident of the state where the application for naturalization is filed for at least three months. If the applicant spent more than one full year during the five year qualifying period outside the U.S., he or she is not eligible for citizenship under the same guidelines.

If the applicant was granted permanent residence based on marriage to a U.S. citizen, he or she can apply for naturalization after three years. However, the following conditions must be met:

✔ The spouse must have been a citizen for three years, <u>and</u>

✔ The couple must have been married for at least three years.

✔ The applicant must have lived in the U.S. for at least eighteen months out of the three years, and

✔ The applicant must have been a resident of the state for at least three months.

The application is filed with the INS in the * state where the alien lives, and can be filed up to three months in advance of actual eligibility. It consists of:

---

1. Form N-400-Application for Naturalization
2. Fingerprints
3. Photographs
4. Copy of front and back of your green card
5. Applicable filing fee
6. Stamped, self addressed envelope for return of filing receipt

---

*Applicants for citizenship in the Los Angeles and New York districts should send their applications directly to their respective INS Regional Service Center.

The applicant will then be called for an interview at the INS. It may take up to eight months to receive the notice. At the interview, the applicant will be asked a series of questions to determine good moral character, the ability to read, write and speak elementary English and the intention to reside in the U.S. permanently. (Aliens over the age of fifty five who have been living in the U.S. as permanent residents for at least fifteen years can have the English language requirement waived. Aliens who are over the age of fifty and have been permanent residents for at least twenty years can also have this requirement waived.) The applicant will also be tested for a basic understanding of U.S. history and the U.S. government, including their belief in the U.S. constitution. The exam can also be taken as part of a course of study given by an independent organization approved by the INS. If the applicant passes, he or she will be given a certificate, valid for one year. The INS will accept the certificate in lieu of the written exam.

People who are certified by a physician to have physical or developmental disabilities or mental impairments are exempt from the literacy and government/history knowledge requirements.

The application must be approved or denied within four months of the interview. Assuming it is approved, the final swearing-in ceremony will be held the same day, or at a later date, depending on the current procedure at your local INS office. At the time of the swearing-in ceremony, the applicant is required to take the following oath of allegiance to the United States of America, and sign this oath.

I hereby declare, on oath, that I absolutely and entirely renounce and abjure all allegiance and fidelity to any foreign prince, potentate, state or sovereignty of whom or which I have heretofore been a subject or citizen; that I will support and defend the Constitution and laws of the United States of America against all enemies, foreign and domestic; that I will bear true faith and allegiance to the same; * that I will bear arms on behalf of the United States when required by law; * that I will perform noncombatant service in the Armed Forces of the United States when required by law; that I will perform work of national importance under civilian direction when required by law; and that I take this obligation freely without any mental reservation or purpose of evasion; so help me God.

* In some cases, the INS will allow these clauses to be omitted.

At the end of the ceremony the applicant is granted a Certificate of Naturalization. This can then be presented at a U.S. Passport Agency office to obtain a U.S. passport. During the naturalization process, the applicant retains his or her U.S. permanent resident status.

For more information on U.S. citizenship, please obtain a copy of our book **Citizenship Made Simple, an easy to read guide to the U.S. citizenship process**. This book can be ordered through your local bookstore or by using the order form provided in the back of this book.

11 IRCA EMPLOYER OBLIGATIONS AND VERIFICATION OF EMPLOYMENT

In 1986, the Immigration Reform and Control Act (IRCA) was established in the U.S. It was developed, in part, to control the number of illegal aliens coming to the U.S. to work. Since the enactment of the program, there have been many controversial issues and regulatory changes. The Immigration Act of 1990 brought about even further changes.

IRCA requires that employers check the identity and the right to work of all new hires (including U.S. citizens), and complete Form I-9- Employment Eligibility Verification for every employee, regardless of their nationality. These regulations also state that the employer cannot discriminate against potential hires on the basis of their origin or citizenship. Form I-9 must be completed for all employees hired after November 6, 1986. Processing and record keeping of Forms I-9 are as follows:

✔ The employee completes Section 1 of the form when he or she starts to work.

✔ The employer reviews the documents that establish the employees right to work and his or her identity and completes Section 2 within three business days of hire. (Lists of documents that the employer can accept to prove identity and the right to work are given later in this chapter.) If the employee cannot produce the documents, but can produce an application receipt for them, this should be recorded, and the employee has 90 days to present the actual document. Section 2 of Form I-9 should be amended at that time. Note that special rules apply to the completion of Form I-9 for minors (under age 18) and handicapped employees.

✔ The employer keeps all Forms I-9 for three years after the employee starts to work, or one year after the employee leaves the employer, whichever is later.

✔ Employers must reverify employment authorization for those employees who initially produced documents with an expiration date, and complete Section 3 on Form I-9. If updated proof of work authorization cannot be provide, the employer cannot continue to employ that individual.

✔ The employer must have all Forms I-9 available to be inspected by an INS officer, or related official. Three days notice should be given.

An employer cannot require that the employee present different documents, or more documents, nor refuse to accept documents that appear to be genuine. Forms I-9 can be photocopied, or the employer can order several copies from: Superintendent of Documents, U.S. Government Printing Office, Washington, DC 20402 Following are lists of acceptable documents:

List A: Employment Eligibility and Identity

1) U.S. passport (even if it has expired)

2) Certificate of U.S. citizenship (Form N-560 or N-561)

3) Certificate of Naturalization (Form N-550 or N-570)

4) Valid foreign passport with a valid I-551 stamp or Form I-94 indicating valid employment authorization

5) Alien Registration Receipt Card (Form I-151 or I-551), which contains a photo of the alien- (i.e. green card)

6) Unexpired Temporary Resident Card (Form I-688)

7) Unexpired Employment Authorization Card (INS Form I-688A)

8) Unexpired Reentry Permit (Form I-327)

9) Unexpired Refugee Travel Document (Form I-571)

10) Unexpired Employment Authorization Document issued by the INS with photo (Form I-688B)

These ten documents establish both employment eligibility and identity. If the employee can produce one of these documents, they have satisfied both the identity and employment eligibility requirement to complete Form I-9:

List B: Identity

1) Driver's license or identification card issued by a state or possession of the U.S., which contains a photo or personal information such as name, birth date, eye color

2) Identification card issued by a Federal, State or Local government agency, which contains a photo or personal information as indicated above (includes U.S. Citizen ID Card- INS Form I-197 and ID Card for use of Resident Citizen in the U.S.- INS Form I-179

3) School identification card with a photo

4) Voter registration card

5) U.S. military card or draft records

6) Military dependent's identification card

7) U.S. Coast Guard Merchant Marine Card

8) Native American Tribal Document

9) Driver's license issued by the Canadian government

10) Non-driver's ID Card issued by a state.

The previous ten documents establish <u>only</u> identity for employees over the age of eighteen. If the employee can produce one of these documents <u>and</u> one document from List C, he or she has satisfied the identity and employment eligibility requirement for completing Form I-9:

<u>List C: Employment Eligibility</u>

1) U.S. Social Security Card (if it states that it is "not valid for employment", it cannot be accepted)

2) Certification of Birth Abroad that is issued by the U.S. Department of State on Form FS-545 or Form DS-1350

3) Original or certified copy of a birth certificate issued by the U.S. and bearing an official seal

4) Native American Tribal Document

5) U.S. Citizen identification card (Form I-197)

6) Identification card for use of Resident Citizen in the U.S. (Form I-179)

7) Valid employment authorization document, issued by the INS (other than those in List A).

8) Form I-797: This is the INS form issued when a petition is approved for nonimmigrant "H","L","O","P","Q" and "R" status and for change of status to "E". Aliens in these categories are only authorized to work for the employers who petitioned for them. The bottom half of this form, together with Form I-94, can be accepted as an employment document under List C.

9) Form I-20ID Copy: This document consists of pages 3 and 4 of the Form I-20, (the certificate of eligibility issued by a school to permit a foreign student to attend that school). Some foreign students may have their work authorization endorsed on this form. Form I-20ID together with Form I-94, showing that a student was admitted for D/S, can be accepted as an employment authorization document under List C.

10) Form IAP-66: Some J-1 exchange visitors have permission to work. Their Form IAP-66 will show this. Form IAP-66, together with Form I-94, is considered an employment authorization document under List C.

The ten documents listed above establish employment eligibility only. As indicated above, one document from List C must be produced with one document from List B.

Note: Certain documents including the U.S. Citizen ID card, Resident Citizen ID card and Native American Tribal Document appear on both List B and List C. These documents can be presented to establish both identity <u>and</u> employment eligibility and should be recorded in both spaces on Form I-9. They are not included in List A, only because they have not been designated by Congress in the law.

The INS has proposed changes to the List of I-9 documents, but as of this publication the rule has not been finalized. Those proposed changes are as follows:

Eliminate from List A:

> Employment authorization card Form I-688A
> Reentry permit
> Refugee travel document

Eliminate from List B:

> School ID card
> Voter's registration card
> U.S. military card or draft record
> Military dependent's ID card
> U.S. Coast Guard Merchant Mariner card
> Identity documents for persons under age 18

Eliminate from List C:

> Birth certification issued by the Department of State
> U.S. citizen ID card

Hiring or continuing to hire aliens who do not have work authorization; failure to complete I-9 forms; and/or unlawful discrimination can result in severe penalties including escalating monetary fines, and in some cases imprisonment.

12 QUESTIONS AND ANSWERS

Over the years, we have been asked many questions about various aspects of processing visas and related matters involving international relocation. We thought that it would be helpful to include some of these questions so that you may benefit from the answers as well.

Q. *Do I need to retain an attorney to assist me in processing my immigration papers and how can I find one to help me?*

A. In most cases, you will need an attorney. The immigration process in the U.S. is extremely complex recent changes make it even more so. There are always administrative changes taking place at the INS offices. If papers are not prepared and filed properly, the odds for a successful outcome are greatly diminished.

Most aliens have friends who have sought immigration counsel in the past and may be able to provide you with the name of a qualified attorney. The **Directory of Immigration Lawyers** is in this book to assist you. The local office of the state Bar Association can also be a helpful source of referral, as can the Legal Aid Society. Many attorneys also advertise their services in the Yellow Pages of the Telephone Directory.

One fact to keep in mind is that not every attorney is as qualified as the next to give you advice on immigration matters. Consult with at least two attorneys and choose the one with whom you feel most comfortable. Make sure to find out before retaining the lawyer what his or her legal fee will be and exactly what the fee will include - e.g., filing fees, miscellaneous expenses such as copy charges and postage. These disbursements can add up quickly! Ask the attorney about the billing schedule so that you can budget your money through the various stages of your immigration case.

Never retain the services of a lawyer who promises or guarantees you anything, or who gives you time frames that seem unrealistic. Do not hesitate to change from one lawyer to another during your case, if you are unhappy with the services being provided. Make sure to obtain your complete file to ensure an easy transition from one lawyer to the next.

Q. *Will the INS be a good source of information on processing my immigration case?*

A. In most situations, calling or visiting the INS will not be very helpful unless you just need general information. The INS employees are very busy and usually do not have the time to plan individual immigration strategies. You may also be putting yourself in jeopardy if you are in the U.S. illegally.

Q. *Where can I obtain immigration forms without visiting the INS?*

A. The easiest way to obtain forms is to call 1-800-870-FORMS.

Q. *Why is my green card case taking so long compared to my friend's?*

A. Do not compare your case with those of friends or relatives. In most instances the facts are not the same, even though they may appear to be. In addition, there are a variety of reasons why identical cases may vary in timing. Your attorney is going to be interested in completing your case as quickly as possible.

Q. *What if I do not have all of the personal documents that are required to complete my case?*

A. The INS and the Consular officials are very strict in this matter. It is almost always possible to obtain duplicate originals of any document that was lost or destroyed. Ask your attorney how to do so. For example, some countries do not issue birth certificates. In these cases, the authorities will accept secondary evidence of birth in the form of affidavits from close relatives. However, the INS and Consular officials maintain books that list which documents are available from each country. If you go to a visa interview without all of the required documents, there is a good chance that your case will be delayed or denied.

Q. *What if a visa appointment is scheduled for me at the INS or at the Consular office and I cannot keep it?*

A. It is very difficult to reschedule appointments because of the heavy volume of cases that these offices must process, and delays of several months can result if requests for rescheduling are made. Do not attempt to change appointment dates unless you absolutely must. In addition, never ignore a notice to appear for an interview at the INS.

Q. *If I have filed an Application for Adjustment of Status from a temporary visa to permanent residence through an Immigration office in the U.S., can I travel while the application is pending?*

A. Once you have filed for permanent residence, your temporary visa should not be used for travel purposes. If you need to travel outside the U.S. during this process for critical business or personal reasons such as a family emergency abroad, you can apply to the INS for a travel document known as an Advance Parole. Use Form I-131- Application for Travel Document. This document allows you to leave and reenter the U.S. within a given period of time. You must, however, be prepared to provide the INS with ample evidence of the need to travel.

Q. *If I obtain my green card through labor certification, must I always work for the same employer?*

A. No. At the time that you are granted permanent residence, the sponsoring employer must intend to have you work for them and you must plan to do so. If the employment relationship does not work out after you have started the job, you can seek other employment.

Q. *How can I obtain a work permit?*

A. Work permits are only issued if you are eligible under one of the categories authorized by the law, and described in this book.

Q. *How can I get a Social Security Number?*

A. If you are in the U.S. legally, and have a working visa, Form I-94, or other document authorizing employment in the U.S., you can obtain a number. You must apply in person at the nearest Social Security Administration Office. Bring your passport, Form I-94 and proof of work authorization. You will be asked to complete an application form (Form SS-5). The Social Security Card will be mailed to you within several weeks.

If you are in the U.S. and do not have work authorization, you cannot obtain a Social Security Number. However, if you need an identification number, for example, to open a brokerage account or to purchase investment property in the U.S., you should request Form W-7 from the Internal Revenue Service and apply for a Taxpayer Identification Number.

Q. *If I have a Social Security number can I work in the U.S.?*

A. The Social Security number is not a work permit. You must also have a visa, Form I-94, or other document that proves you have employment authorization.

Q. Am I eligible to collect Social Security?

A. The following classes of individuals are included in those who may be eligible for Social Security benefits: naturalized citizens; permanent resident aliens; temporary residents through a variety of programs including amnesty; refugees and asylees. This list is not all inclusive.

Q. Am I eligible for unemployment benefits?

A. If you are a naturalized U.S. citizen or have permanent work authorization, you may be eligible for unemployment benefits.

Q. How can I obtain a U.S. driver's license?

A. In most states you need proof that you are in the U.S. in legal status. If you are in the U.S. illegally, it is very difficult to obtain a driver's license. It is also difficult to obtain a driver's license if you are in the U.S. as a visitor.

Q. If I give birth to a baby in the U.S., what is the baby's status and can the baby grant me an immigration benefit?

A. The baby is a U.S. citizen by having been born in the U.S. A child cannot pass on an immigration benefit to a parent until the child reaches the age of twenty one.

Q. Should I marry a U.S. citizen solely to obtain a green card?

A. No. Doing so may be illegal. The INS continues to tighten its policy regarding marriages strictly for immigration purposes, and the penalties can be severe. In fact, you should not get involved in any arrangement that is meant to defraud the INS. Remember, the INS is a branch of the U.S. Government and should be treated with respect.

Q. What do I do if I complete my permanent residence application but do not receive my green card in the mail?

A. This is a common occurrence. If you do not receive your card within ninety days of approval of your application, you should follow up with the INS card processing facility (not your local INS office). Obtain Form G-731-Inquiry Concerning Status of I-551, and follow the instructions.

Q. *What happens if I lose my green card or if it is stolen?*

A. A lost or stolen green card can be replaced. When you first receive your card, record your alien registration number and keep it in a safe place. If your green card is lost and you are in the U.S., you must process an application with INS to replace the card. The application consists of Form I-90- Application to Replace Alien Registration Card, photographs and the applicable filing fee. You will need to visit the INS office where you live so that they can take a new fingerprint, which will appear on the updated card. If your green card is stolen, INS may ask that you obtain a police report from your local police station. In either event, once the I-90 is filed, INS will stamp a new temporary green card in your passport so that you can travel. They will then forward the I-90 application to the Immigration Card Facility in Texas for processing of a new card.

If you are outside the U.S. and your card is lost or stolen, go to the nearest American Embassy or Consulate. Your permanent residence will be verified with the Department of State in Washington, DC and you will be issued a document to allow you to return to the U.S. This can sometimes take several days. Once you are back in the U.S., you will need to file an I-90 application as described above.

Q. *If I received my green card as a young child do I need to update it?*

A. Yes. If your card was issued before the age of fourteen it must be updated to include fingerprints. Take your card to the nearest immigration office and complete an I-90 application as described above. The INS will fingerprint you and take new photos and a new card will subsequently be issued from the Immigration Card Facility in Texas. The INS should stamp a temporary green card in your passport so that you can travel outside the U.S. while you are waiting for the new card.

Q. *Can I keep my green card if I am not living in the U.S.?*

A. If you are temporarily residing outside the U.S. but continue to consider the U.S. your permanent home, and plan to return permanently, it is possible to keep your green card. However, you must comply with several INS rules. These rules are complex and you should consult a professional for advice. You can also apply to the INS for a Permit to Reenter the United States using Form I-131- Application for Travel Document. The granting of this permit allows you to remain outside the U.S. for up to two years without jeopardizing your permanent resident status. Your absence from the U.S. for more than one year however, can still affect your ability to apply for U.S. citizenship.

Q. *Does my green card need to be renewed or does it remain valid forever?*

A. In 1989 the Alien Registration Card regulations were revised by the INS. The card used to be valid as long as the alien remained a permanent resident. Now the card expires ten years after the date it was issued. The alien will then be required to obtain a new card. In addition, all Alien Registration Cards issued before 1978 must be replaced with new cards.

Q. *What if I am in the United States illegally, can I still adjust my status in the United States?*

A. Under certain circumstances you may be allowed to adjust your status. There have been recent changes in the law, however, that may affect your application. Consult a professional before you file any applications.

13 DIRECTORY OF IMMIGRATION LAWYERS

There are many areas of specialization within the legal profession in the U.S. A lawyer who concentrates on immigration matters will have a better understanding of your objectives as they relate to the ever changing regulations of our system. The following is a list, alphabetically by state, of lawyers who specialize in immigration matters. The Directory also contains listings outside the continental U.S. Interview the attorneys, discuss their level of expertise and inquire about fees in advance. ***Please mention that you obtained the lawyer's name from this book.*** The authors do not personally know all of these attorneys, and cannot be held responsible for the accuracy of the advice given by them.

LAWYERS WITHIN THE CONTINENTAL UNITED STATES

ARIZONA

JOANNE STARK
HIRSON WEXLER PERL & STARK
3443 NORTH CENTRAL AVENUE, SUITE 706
PHOENIX, ARIZONA 85012
TELEPHONE: (602) 266-4700, FAX: (602) 266-8108

WILLIAM E. MORGA
MORGA LAW OFFICES
7000 E. SHEA BOULEVARD, #110
SCOTTSDALE, ARIZONA 85254
TELEPHONE: (602) 991-9565, FAX: (602) 991-9552

CALIFORNIA

DAVID HIRSON, ESQ., MANAGING PARTNER
HIRSON, WEXLER PERL & STARK
ONE PARK PLAZA, SUITE 950
IRVINE, CALIFORNIA 92614
TELEPHONE: (714) 251-8844, FAX: (714) 251-1545

MITCHELL L. WEXLER, ESQ.
HIRSON, WEXLER PERL & STARK
6310 SAN VICENTE BOULEVARD, SUITE 415
LOS ANGELES, CALIFORNIA 90048
TELEPHONE: (213) 936-0200, FAX: (213) 936-4488

GARY B. PERL, ESQ.
HIRSON, WEXLER PERL & STARK
8899 UNIVERSITY CENTER LANE, SUITE 310
SAN DIEGO, CALIFORNIA 92122
TELEPHONE: (619) 452-5700, FAX: (619) 452-1911

California Continued on Next Page

ARNOLD S. MALTER
LAW OFFICES OF ARNOLD S. MALTER
660 S. FIGUEROA STREET, 22ND FLOOR
LOS ANGELES, CALIFORNIA 90017
TELEPHONE: (213) 622-3636, FAX: (213) 622-3331

ROBERT L. LEWIS, ATTORNEY
LAW OFFICE OF ROBERT L. LEWIS
500 SANSOME STREET, SUITE 614
SAN FRANCISCO, CALIFORNIA 94111
TELEPHONE: (415) 362-1288, FAX: (415) 362-0332

JIHAD H. CHAMMAS, MANAGING ATTORNEY
LAW OFFICES OF JIHAD H. CHAMMAS
1055 WILSHIRE BOULEVARD, SUITE 1996
LOS ANGELES, CALIFORNIA 90017
TELEPHONE: (213) 250-4400; FAX: (213) 250-4468

NANCY FULLER-JACOBS
LUCE, FORWARD, HAMILTON & SCRIPPS
600 WEST BROADWAY, SUITE 2600
SAN DIEGO, CALIFORNIA 92101
TELEPHONE: (619) 699-2444, FAX: (619) 232-8311

ROBERT G. WERNER
WERNER & ASSOCIATES
690 MARKET STREET, SUITE #1006
SAN FRANCISCO, CALIFORNIA 94104
TELEPHONE: (415) 981-7932, FAX: (415) 981-7997

GINA DARVAS, ATTORNEY
LAW OFFICE OF GINA DARVAS
1094 CUDAHY PL, SUITE 214
SAN DIEGO, CALIFORNIA 92110
TELEPHONE: (619) 275-7574, FAX: (619) 275-7562

JULIE PEARL, MANAGING ATTORNEY
MUNRO, NELSON & PEARL
FIRST MARKET TOWER 525 MARKET STREET, 34TH FLOOR
SAN FRANCISCO, CALIFORNIA 94105
TELEPHONE: (415) 771-7500, FAX: (415) 771-5009

LEON J. SNAID
LAW OFFICES OF LEON J. SNAID
6265 GREENWICH DRIVE, SUITE 103
SAN DIEGO, CALIFORNIA 92122
TELEPHONE: (619) 638-9086, FAX: (619) 638-9083

MEREDITH BROWN, LEGAL DIRECTOR
ONE STOP IMMIGRATION & EDUCATIONAL CENTER, INC.
3600 WHITTIER BOULEVARD
LOS ANGELES, CALIFORNIA 90023
TELEPHONE: (213) 268-8472, FAX: (213) 268-2231

California Continued on Next Page

HALEH MANSOURI, OWNER
LAW OFFICES OF HALEH MANSOURI
624 S. GRAND AVENUE SUITE 2100
LOS ANGELES, CALIFORNIA 90017
TELEPHONE: (213) 489-7120, FAX: (213) 489-7122

HELEN Y.H. HUI, ATTORNEY AT LAW
456 MONTGOMERY STREET, SUITE 700
SAN FRANCISCO, CALIFORNIA 94104-1240
TELEPHONE: (415) 781-8251, FAX: (415) 434-3748

COLORADO

LAURA L. KORKIN
LAURA KORKIN & ASSOCIATES, P.C.
1503 SPRUCE STREET, SUITE 1
BOULDER, COLORADO 80302
TELEPHONE: (303) 545-9665, FAX: (303) 545-9667

LISA E. BATTAN
LAURA KORKIN & ASSOCIATES, P.C.
1503 SPRUCE STREET, SUITE 1
BOULDER, COLORADO 80302
TELEPHONE: (303) 545-9665, FAX: (303) 545-9667

JIM SALVATOR, ATTORNEY AT LAW
1643 ERIN WAY
LAFAYETTE, COLORADO 80026
TELEPHONE: (303) 604-0320, FAX: (303) 604-2024

CONNECTICUT

ROBERT A. MARESCA, ATTORNEY AT LAW
ANTIGNANI & MARESCA, P.C.
275 CONGRESS STREET
BRIDGEPORT, CONNECTICUT 06604
TELEPHONE: (203) 367-8437, FAX: (203) 339-4300

DISTRICT OF COLUMBIA (WASHINGTON, D.C.)

GLEN D. WASSERSTEIN, ESQUIRE
IMMIGRATION LAW GROUP, P.C.
2000 L STREET, NW, SUITE 200
WASHINGTON, DC 20036
TELEPHONE: (202) 416-1789, FAX: (202) 416-1719

ARNULFO CHAPA, PRESIDENT
CHAPA LAW OFFICES, P.C.
804 TUCKERMAN STREET, NW
WASHINGTON, DC 20011
TELEPHONE: (202) 882-1068, FAX: (202) 829-6074

Washington Continued on Next Page

KATHY A. LIEBERMAN, PARTNER (SPANISH)
LIEBERMAN & MARK
729 15TH STREET, NW, 2ND FLOOR
WASHINGTON, DC 20005
TELEPHONE: (202) 393-3020, FAX: (202) 393-8350

SHEILA T. STARKEY, ATTORNEY
MARTY, LAMADRID & STARKEY
1225 I ST, NW, SUITE 500
WASHINGTON, DC. 20005
TELEPHONE: (202) 682-4724, FAX: (202) 682-5844

FLORIDA

DAVID B. ETHERINGTON, ATTORNEY AT LAW
ETHERINGTON & CHAMBLIS, P.A.
2830 NW 41ST STREET, SUITE L
GAINESVILLE, FLORIDA 32606
TELEPHONE: (904) 377-1302, FAX: (904) 377-1169

WALLACE J.D. WEYLIE
WALLACE J.D. WEYLIE LAW OFFICE
350 GULF BOULEVARD
INDIAN ROCKS BEACH, FLORIDA 33785
TELEPHONE: (813) 596-9078, FAX: (813) 593-2192

MANJULA KALIDINDI
LAW OFFICES OF MANJULA KALIDINDI
300 SOUTH PINE ISLAND ROAD, SUITE 235
PLANTATION, FLORIDA 33324
TELEPHONE: (954) 723-9105, FAX: (954) 723-9106

SANDRA LAMBERT, ESQUIRE
SANDRA LAMBERT, P.A.
370 W. CAMINO GARDENS BOULEVARD, SUITE 117
BOCA RATON, FLORIDA 33432
TELEPHONE: (561) 368-0268, FAX: (561) 394-2970

PETER J. JAENSCH
AMERICAN IMMIGRATION SERVICES, INC.
3400 S. TAMIAMI TRAIL, #303
SARASOTA, FLORIDA 34239
TELEPHONE: (941) 365-VISA OR 8472, FAX: (941) 923-8356

CAROLINE R. VOS, ATTORNEY AT LAW
LAW OFFICES OF CAROLINE VOS
8875 HIDDEN RIVER PARKWAY, SUITE 300
TAMPA, FLORIDA 33637
TELEPHONE: (813) 975-7263, FAX: (813) 975-7264

Florida Continued on Next Page

GLADYS GONZALEZ-BOYER, ESQ.
GONZALEZ-BOYER & EXPOSITO, P.A.
10621 N. KENDALL DRIVE, SUITE 208
MIAMI, FLORIDA, 33176
TELEPHONE: (305) 595-5553 FAX: (305) 595-8313

JODI B. GREEN, ESQ.
JODI B. GREEN, P.A.
1499 WEST PALMETTO PARK ROAD, SUITE 300
BOCA RATON, FLORIDA 33486
TELEPHONE: (561) 391-3221, FAX: (561) 392-2611)

GEORGIA

JAMES M. DUNN, ATTORNEY AT LAW
102 BOMBAY LANE
ROSWELL, GEORGIA 30076
TELEPHONE: (770) 754-6230, FAX: (770) 754-6232

ILLINOIS

ROYAL F. BERG, ATTORNEY AT LAW
33 NORTH LASALLE, SUITE 2300
CHICAGO, ILLINOIS 60602
TELEPHONE: (312) 855-1118

SCOTT D. POLLOCK
SCOTT D. POLLOCK & ASSOCIATES
20 N. WACKER DRIVE, SUITE 3330
CHICAGO, ILLINOIS 60606
TELEPHONE: (312)444-1940, FAX: (312) 444-1950

D0UGLAS BRISTOL
LAW OFFICES OF DOUGLAS BRISTOL
321 SOUTH PLYMOUTH COURT, SUITE 1525
CHICAGO, ILLINOIS 60604-3912
TELEPHONE: (312) 663-4466, FAX: (312) 663-5252

LYNNE R. FELDMAN, ATTORNEY AT LAW
ERWIN, MARTINKUS & COLE LTD
411 W. UNIVERSITY AVENUE
CHAMPAIGN, ILLINOIS 61820
TELEPHONE: (217) 351-4040, FAX: (217) 351-4314

T.V. WEBER, ESQ.
31 W. DOWNER PLACE
AURORA, ILLINOIS 60506
TELEPHONE: (630) 264-8230, FAX: (630) 264-8231

INDIANA

JERRI L. MEAD, ATTORNEY AT LAW
5525A COLDWATER ROAD, SUITE 104
FORT WAYNE, INDIANA 46825
TELEPHONE: (219) 426-4337, FAX: (219) 422-6622

KANSAS

SANDRINE LISK-ANANI
IMMIGRATION LAW OFFICE
PO BOX 49462
WICHITA, KANSAS 67201-9462
TELEPHONE: (316) 262-6222, FAX: (316) 262-6323

KENTUCKY

DAN L. OWENS, MEMBER
BROWN, TODD & HEYBURN PLLC
400 WEST MARKET, 3200 PROVIDIAN TOWER
LOUISVILLE, KENTUCKY 40202
TELEPHONE: (502) 589-5400; FAX: (502) 581-1087

DOUGLAS S. WEIGLE, ESQ.
BARTLETT & WEIGLE CO., PSC
121 EAST FOURTH STREET
COVINGTON, KY 41011
TELEPHONE: (606) 491-5500, FAX: (606) 491-5544

MAINE

GEORGE D. HEPNER, III, ATTORNEY
LAW OFFICE OF GEORGE D. HEPNER, III
765 CONGRESS STREET, THIRD FLOOR
PORTLAND, MAINE 04102
TELEPHONE: (207) 828-0042

MICHAEL A. DUDDY, ESQ.
KOZAK, GAYER & BRODEK, P.A.
15 COLUMBIA STREET
BANGOR, MAINE 04401
TELEPHONE: (207) 990-4800, FAX: (207) 990-4804

MARYLAND

JEANY MARK, PARTNER (CHINESE)
LIEBERMAN & MARK
6701 DEMOCRACY BLVD, #300
BETHESDA, MARYLAND 20817
TELEPHONE: (301) 309-8070

MARIA F. GLINSMANN, ESQ.
GLINSMANN & GLINSMANN, CHARTERED
702 RUSSELL AVENUE, SUITE 312
GAITHERSBURG, MARYLAND 20877
TELEPHONE: (301) 548-0550, FAX: (301) 548-0553

MASSACHUSETTS

RODNEY M. BARKER, ESQ.
BARKER & LOSCOCCO, P.C.
TEN WINTHROP SQUARE
BOSTON, MASSACHUSETTS 02110
TELEPHONE: (617) 482-4900, FAX: (617) 426-5251

JOHN J.LOSCOCCO, ESQ.
BARKER & LOSCOCCO, P.C.
TEN WINTHROP SQUARE
BOSTON, MASSACHUSETTS 02110
TELEPHONE: (617) 482-4900, FAX: (617) 426-5251

RICHARD L. IANDOLI, ESQ.
LAW OFFICES OF IANDOLI & ASSOCIATES
36 MELROSE STREET
BOSTON, MASSACHUSETTS 02116
TELEPHONE: (617) 482-1010, FAX: (617) 423-9070

MARIA H. LAWCEWICZ, ATTORNEY
LAW OFFICE OF MARIA H. LAWCEWICZ
14 BEACON STREET, SUITE 814
BOSTON, MASSACHUSETTS 02108
TELEPHONE: (617) 723-6847, FAX: (617) 723-2040

MARIA JOSE MARTY, ATTORNEY
MARTY, LAMADRID & STARKEY
TEN POST OFFICE SQUARE, SUITE 600 SOUTH
BOSTON, MASSACHUSETTS 02109
TELEPHONE: (617) 576-9539, FAX: (617) 576-9550

MICHIGAN

ALEXANDRA V. LACOMBE, ESQ.
ALEXANDR V. LACOMBE, P.C.
37727 PROFESSIONAL CENTER DR., SUITE 125D
LIVONIA, MI 48154
TELEPHONE: (313) 432-0506, FAX: (313) 432-0502

MINNESOTA

LESLIE A. KARAM
LUBINER & KARAM
2950 METRO DRIVE, SUITE 314
BLOOMINGTON, MINNESOTA 55425
TELEPHONE: (612) 854-3313, FAX: (612) 854-2033

MISSISSIPPI

THOMAS J. ROSSER
BLACK, BOBANGO & MORGAN
530 OAK COURT DRIVE, SUITE 345
MEMPHIS, TENNESSEE 38117
TELEPHONE: (901) 762-0530, FAX: (601) 349-0888

MISSOURI

ANDREA FOX SCHWARTZ, ESQ.
16353 WILSON FARM DRIVE
CHESTERFIELD, MISSOURI 63005
TELEPHONE: (314) 530-6127, FAX: (314) 530-6127

MONTANA

JAMES P. SITES, ATTORNEY
CROWLEY, HAUGHEY, HANSON, TOOLE & DIETRICH
490 NORTH 31ST STREET, PO BOX 2529
BILLINGS, MONTANA 59103
TELEPHONE: (406) 252-3441, FAX: (406) 256-8526

DEBORAH S. SMITH
REYNOLDS, MOFL AND SHERWOOD
401 N. LAST CHANCE GULCH
HELENA, MONTANA 59601
TELEPHONE: (406) 442-3261, FAX: (406) 443-7294

NEBRASKA

VARD R. JOHNSON, ATTORNEY
BROOM, JOHNSON AND CLARKSON
310 FLATIRON BUILDING
OMAHA, NEBRASKA 68102
TELEPHONE: (402) 346-8323, FAX: (402) 346-5426

NEW JERSEY

ALAN M. LUBINER
LUBINER & SCHMIDT
515 N. MICHIGAN AVENUE
KENILWORTH, NEW JERSEY 07033
TELEPHONE: (908) 688-5100, FAX: (908) 688-6211

ANTHONY F SILIATO, PARTNER
MEYNER AND LANDIS
ONE GATEWAY CENTER
NEWARK, NEW JERSEY 07102
TELEPHONE: (973) 624-2800, FAX: (973) 624-0356

JAYSHREE J. PATEL, ATTORNEY AT LAW
LAW OFFICE OF JAYSHREE PATEL
921 BERGEN AVENUE, SUITE 928
JERSEY CITY, NEW JERSEY 07306
TELEPHONE: (201) 659-0330, FAX: (201) 659-2473

DAVID H. NACHMAN, ESQ. MANAGING ATTORNEY
NACHMAN & GROHMANN, P.C.
17 ARCADIAN AVENUE, SUITE 208
PARAMUS, NEW JERSEY 07652
TELEPHONE: (201) 587-8200, FAX: (201) 587-0587

FREDERICK A. ORGAN, ESQ.
ORGAN & STRAWINSKI
649 WESTWOOD AVENUE
RIVER VALE, NEW JERSEY 07675
TELEPHONE: (201) 666-8700, FAX: (201) 666-0943

VRAT PECHOTA, JR., ESQ.
LAW OFFICES OF VRATISLAV PECHOTA, JR.
36 KETLEY PLACE
PRINCETON, NEW JERSEY 08540
TELEPHONE: (609) 734-0174, FAX: (609) 734-0174

NEVADA

JOANNE T. STARK, ESQ.
HIRSON WEXLER PERL & STARK
3753 HOWARD HUGHES PARKWAY, SUITE 200
LAS VEGAS, NEVADA 89109
TELEPHONE: (702) 737-5414, FAX: (702) 792-5107

NEW YORK

RAJ BHUSHAN, ATTORNEY AND COUNSELOR AT LAW
2793 BRIGHTON 8TH STREET
BROOKLYN, NEW YORK 11235
TELEPHONE: (718)891-9802, FAX: (718) 891-4746

JEFFREY A. FEINBLOOM, COUNSELOR AT LAW
THE EMPIRE STATE BUILDING, 350 FIFTH AVENUE, SUITE 6101
NEW YORK, NEW YORK 10118
TELEPHONE: (212) 279-5299, FAX: (212) 643-8182

NEIL H. AFRAN, ESQ.
AFRAN & RUSSO, P.C.
300 RABRO DRIVE, SUITE 116
HAUPPAUGE, NEW YORK 11788-4256
TELEPHONE: (516) 582-5753, FAX: (516) 582-5754

ANIELLA RUSSO, ESQ.
AFRAN & RUSSO, P.C.
300 RABRO DRIVE, SUITE 116
HAUPPAUGE, NEW YORK 11788-4256
TELEPHONE: (516) 582-5753, FAX: (516) 582-5754

CHRISTINE GIULINI, ESQ.
GIULINI & GIULINI
475 FIFTH AVENUE, SUITE 602
NEW YORK, NEW YORK 10017
TELEPHONE: (212) 725-5411, FAX: (212) 545- 7211

LOUISE S. CAVANAUGH, ESQ.
LOUISE CAVANAUGH, LAW OFFICES
450 7TH AVENUE, SUITE 2209
NEW YORK, NEW YORK 10123
TELEPHONE: (212)760-2772, FAX: (212)947-8339

VRAT PECHOTA, JR., ESQ.
LAW OFFICES OF VRATISLAV PECHOTA, JR.
225 WEST 34TH STREET, #1806
NEW YORK, NEW YORK 10122
TELEPHONE: (212) 268-4969, FAX: (212) 244-0355

JOTHAM S. J0HANN, MEMBER NY, NY, CT, PA BARS
JOHANN & ASSOCIATES
1900 HEMPSTEAD TURNPIKE, SUITE 200
EAST MEADOW, NEW YORK 11554
TELEPHONE: (516) 794-2537, FAX: (516) 794-6535

ALEXANDRA V. TSEITLIN, ATTORNEY AT LAW
LAW OFFICE OF ALEXANDRA V. TSEITLIN
310 MADISON AVENUE, SUITE 1905
NEW YORK, NY 10017
TELEPHONE: (212 692-9282, FAX: (212) 953-0447

NORTH CAROLINA

PENNI P. BRADSHAW, ATTORNEY
KILPATRICK STOCKTON LLP
1001 WEST FOURTH STREET
WINSTON-SALEM, NORTH CAROLINA 27101-2400
TELEPHONE: (910) 607-7444, FAX: (910) 607-7505

CHRISTINA E. LANG, ATTORNEY
CHAPMAN & ASSOCIATES
404-A NORTH EUGENE STREET
GREENSBORO, NORTH CAROLINA 27401
TELEPHONE: (910) 334-0034, FAX: (910) 334-0036

GERARD M. CHAPMAN, ATTORNEY
CHAPMAN & ASSOCIATES
404-A NORTH EUGENE STREET
GREENSBORO, NORTH CAROLINA 27401
TELEPHONE: (910) 334-0034, FAX: (910) 334-0036

KAREN FRASIER ALSTON, ATTORNEY AT LAW
THE LAW OFFICES OF JAMES D. WILLIAMS, JR. P.A.
3400 CROASDAILE DRIVE, SUITE 205
DURHAM, NORTH CAROLINA 27705
TELEPHONE: 1 (800) 539-1114, (919) 382-8115, FAX: (919) 382-7413

OHIO

J. RYAN HUTTON,E SQ.
MARKEY, HUTTON & POWERS, L.L.C
36 EAST FOURTH STREET, SUITE 1208
CINCINNATI, OHIO 45202
TELEPHONE: (513) 621-1114; FAX: (513) 621-4694

PETER B. LI, ATTORNEY
LAW OFFICE OF ATTORNEY PETER B. LI
THE ARCADE, 401 EUCLID AVENUE, SUITE 353
CLEVELAND, OHIO 44114-2402
TELEPHONE: (216) 771-8277, FAX: (216) 771-8278

DOUGLAS S. WEIGLE, ESQ.
BARTLETT & WEIGLE CO., L.P.A.
432 WALNUT STREET, SUITE 1100
CINCINNATI, OHIO 45202
TELEPHONE: (513) 241-3992, FAX: (513) 241-1816

SAM SHIHAB, PARTNER
GOLDMAN, SHIHAB & SHIHAB
500 SOUTH FRONT STREET, SUITE 1140
COLUMBUS, OHIO 43215
TELEPHONE: (614) 224-2428, FAX: (614) 224-5080

Ohio Continued on Next Page

UCHE MGBARAHO, ESQ., ATTORNEY AT LAW
1677 E 40TH STREET
CLEVELAND, OHIO 44103
TELEPHONE: (216)881-1220, FAX: (216) 881-5039

MARGARET W. WONG, ATTORNEY AT LAW
MARGARET W. WONG & ASSOC. CO., LPA
1370 ONTARIO STREET, SUITE 1128
CLEVELAND, OHIO 44113
TELEPHONE: (216) 566-9908, FAX: (216) 566-1125

DONALD C. SLOWIK, ESQ.
LAW OFFICES OF DONALD C. SLOWIK
341 SOUTH THIRD STREET, SUITE 10
COLUMBUS, OHIO 43215
TELEPHONE: (614) 224-3122, FAX: (614) 224-9486

OKLAHOMA

TURNER PRIMROSE, ATTORNEY AT LAW
PRIMROSE LAW OFFICE
115 S. PETERS
NORMAN, OKLAHOMA 73069
TELEPHONE: (405) 321-6004, FAX: (405) 366-2896

TURNER PRIMROSE, ATTORNEY AT LAW
PRIMROSE LAW OFFICE
5801 E. 41ST, SUITE 801, LOCAL AMERICA BANK BUILDING
TULSA, OKLAHOMA
TELEPHONE: (918) 665-3003, FAX: (405) 366-2896

TURNER PRIMROSE, ATTORNEY AT LAW
PRIMROSE LAW OFFICE
4300 HIGHLINE BOULEVARD, SUITE 222
OKLAHOMA CITY, OKLAHOMA 73108
TELEPHONE: (405) 321-6004, FAX: (405) 366-2896

E. VANCE WINNINGHAM, ESQ.
WINNINGHAM & STEIN
2200 NW 50TH, SUITE 240
OKLAHOMA CITY, OKLAHOMA 73112
TELEPHONE: (405) 843-1037, FAX: (405) 848-2463

E. VANCE WINNINGHAM, ESQ.
WINNINGHAM & STEIN
5 WEST 22
TULSA, OKLAHOMA 74114
TELEPHONE: (918) 592-1448

Oklahoma continued on next page

RANCE G. STEIN, ESQ.
WINNINGHAM & STEIN
2200 NW 50TH, SUITE 240
OKLAHOMA CITY, OKLAHOMA 73112
TELEPHONE: (405) 843-1037, FAX: (405) 848-2463

PENNSYLVANIA

WENDY CASTOR HESS
GOLDBLUM & HESS
JENKINTOWN PLAZA, SUITE 380
JENKINTOWN, PENNSYLVANIA 19046
TELEPHONE: (215) 885-3600, FAX: (215) 885-4595

DAVID KAPLAN, ESQUIRE
LAW OFFICES OF DAVID KAPLAN
306 PARSONS AVENUE
BALA CYNWYD, PENNSYLVANIA 19004
TELEPHONE: (888) 3KAPLAN, (610) 667-2742, FAX: (610) 667-2744

TENNESSEE

REHIM BABAOGLU, ATTORNEY AT LAW
BYRD & COBB
99 NORTH THIRD STREET
MEMPHIS, TENNESSEE 38103-2370
TELEPHONE: (901) 523-0301, FAX: (901) 523-0343

BARRY L. FRAGER, ATTORNEY AT LAW
LAW OFFICES OF BARRY L. FRAGER
5100 POPLAR AVENUE, SUITE 2222
MEMPHIS, TENNESSEE 38137
TELEPHONE: (901) 763-3188, FAX: (901) 763-3475

CISA LINXWILER, ATTORNEY AT LAW
LAW OFFICES OF BARRY L. FRAGER
5100 POPLAR AVENUE, SUITE 2222
MEMPHIS, TENNESSEE 38137
TELEPHONE: (901) 763-3188, FAX: (901) 763-3475

THOMAS J. ROSSER
BLACK, BOBANGO & MORGAN
530 OAK COURT DRIVE, SUITE 345
MEMPHIS, TENNESSEE 38117
TELEPHONE: (901) 762-0530, FAX: (901) 683-2553

TEXAS

NANCY TAYLOR SHIVERS
SHIVERS & SHIVERS
1146 S. ALAMO
SAN ANTONIO, TEXAS 78210
TELEPHONE: (210) 226-9725; FAX: (210) 226-4428

ROBERT A. SHIVERS
SHIVERS & SHIVERS
1146 S. ALAMO
SAN ANTONIO, TEXAS 78210
TELEPHONE: (210) 226-9725; FAX: (210) 226-4428

R.V. REDDY, ATTORNEY AT LAW
LAW OFFICES OF R.V. REDDY
7171 HARWIN, #312
HOUSTON, TEXAS 77036
TELEPHONE: (713) 953-7787; FAX: (713) 953-7797

YAN MIN KUO, JD, PHD
YAN MIN KUO & ASSOCIATES
9600 BELLAIRE BOULEVARD, #218
HOUSTON, TEXAS 77036
TELEPHONE: (713) 988-9000; FAX: (713) 721-5888

JAMES OKORAFOR, ESQ.
OKORAFOR AND HUNTER
8303 SOUTH WEST FREEWAY #320
HOUSTON, TEXAS 77074
TELEPHONE: (713) 272-8882, FAX: (713) 272-8883

VIRGINIA

KENNETH J. LASKY, ESQ.
MAGEE, FOSTER, GOLDSTEIN & SAYERS, P.C.
310 FIRST STREET, S.W., SUITE 1200
ROANOKE, VIRGINIA 24011
TELEPHONE: (540) 343-9800, TELECOPY: (540) 343-9898

GLORIA CALONGE, ESQ.
CALONGE, GARCIA & ASSOCIATES
5627 COLUMBIA PIKE, SUITE 200
FALLS CHURCH, VIRGINIA 22041
TELEPHONE: (703) 578-3556; FAX: (703) 578-3557

SYLVIA J. BOECKER, ATTORNEY AT LAW
SYLVIA J. BOECKER, P.C.
732 VIRGINIA DARE DRIVE
VIRGINIA BEACH, VIRGINIA 23451
TELEPHONE: (757) 491-7995; FAX: (757) 491-8986

Virginia continued on next page

ANA M. CUITINO, ATTORNEY AT LAW
ANA M. CUITINO LAW OFFICE, P.C.
3900 N. FAIRFAX DRIVE, SUITE 400
ARLINGTON, VIRGINIA 22203
TELEPHONE: (703) 243-4421, FAX: (703) 243-4543

RAKESH MEHROTRA, ESQ.
KAVRUKOV, MEHROTRA & DIJOSEPH, L.L.P.
2101 WILSON BOULEVARD
ARLINGTON, VIRGINIA 22201
TELEPHONE: (703) 243-2343, FAX: (703) 524-7833

ELIOT NORMAN, DIRECTOR
IMMIGRATION PRACTICE GROUP
MEZZULLO & MCCANDLISH
PO BOX 796, 111 E. MAIN STREET
RICHMOND, VIRGINIA 23218
TELEPHONE: (804) 775-3815, FAX: (804) 775-3816

WISCONSIN

THOMAS C. HOCHSTATTER, ESQ., PARTNER
HOCHSTATTER, MCCARTHY & RIVAS, S.C.
5555 N. PORT WASHINGTON ROAD, SUITE 302
MILWAUKEE, WISCONSIN 53217
TELEPHONE: (414) 962-7440, FAX: (414) 962-0353

GAIL K. MCCARTHY, ESQ., PARTNER
HOCHSTATTER, MCCARTHY & RIVAS, S.C.
5555 N. PORT WASHINGTON ROAD, SUITE 302
MILWAUKEE, WISCONSIN 53217
TELEPHONE: (414) 962-7440, FAX: (414) 962-0353

JOSEPH M. RIVAS, ESQ., PARTNER
HOCHSTATTER, MCCARTHY & RIVAS, S.C.
5555 N. PORT WASHINGTON ROAD, SUITE 302
MILWAUKEE, WISCONSIN 53217
TELEPHONE: (414) 962-7440, FAX: (414) 962-0353

Lawyers Outside the U.S. Listed on Next Page

LAWYERS OUTSIDE THE CONTINENTAL UNITED STATES

PUERTO RICO

ANGUEIRA & ASSOCIATES
1ST BANK BUILDING, 1519 P. DE LEON AVENUE
SUITES 717-718
SAN JUAN, PUERTO RICO 00909
TELEPHONE: (787) 722-3040, FAX: (787) 723-0233

CANADA

GARY E. HANSON
HANSON & COMPANY
280, 521-3 AVENUE, SW
CALGARY AB T2P 3T3
CANADA
TELEPHONE: (403) 261-6890, FAX: (403) 263-1632

14 SAMPLE FORMS

The following pages contain samples of the forms that you will need to process your immigration and labor certification applications. The forms are frequently updated, so the ones included in this book should only be used to give you a general idea of the types of questions you will be asked when preparing applications. The most recent version of each form can usually be obtained by calling the INS office or the Department of Labor, as applicable.

continued on next page

U.S. Department of Justice
Immigration and Naturalization Service

FORM G-325A
BIOGRAPHIC INFORMATION

OMB No. 1115-0066
Approval expires 4-30-85

(Family name)	(First name)	(Middle name)	☐ MALE ☐ FEMALE	BIRTHDATE (Mo.-Day-Yr.)	NATIONALITY	FILE NUMBER A-

ALL OTHER NAMES USED (Including names by previous marriages)		CITY AND COUNTRY OF BIRTH	SOCIAL SECURITY NO. (If any)

	FAMILY NAME	FIRST NAME	DATE, CITY AND COUNTRY OF BIRTH (If known)	CITY AND COUNTRY OF RESIDENCE
FATHER				
MOTHER (Maiden name)				

HUSBAND (If none, so state) OR WIFE	FAMILY NAME (For wife, give maiden name)	FIRST NAME	BIRTHDATE	CITY & COUNTRY OF BIRTH	DATE OF MARRIAGE	PLACE OF MARRIAGE

FORMER HUSBANDS OR WIVES (If none, so state)

FAMILY NAME (For wife, give maiden name)	FIRST NAME	BIRTHDATE	DATE & PLACE OF MARRIAGE	DATE AND PLACE OF TERMINATION OF MARRIAGE

APPLICANT'S RESIDENCE LAST FIVE YEARS. LIST PRESENT ADDRESS FIRST.

STREET AND NUMBER	CITY	PROVINCE OR STATE	COUNTRY	FROM MONTH	FROM YEAR	TO MONTH	TO YEAR
						PRESENT TIME	

APPLICANT'S LAST ADDRESS OUTSIDE THE UNITED STATES OF MORE THAN ONE YEAR

STREET AND NUMBER	CITY	PROVINCE OR STATE	COUNTRY	FROM MONTH	FROM YEAR	TO MONTH	TO YEAR

APPLICANT'S EMPLOYMENT LAST FIVE YEARS. (IF NONE, SO STATE.) LIST PRESENT EMPLOYMENT FIRST

FULL NAME AND ADDRESS OF EMPLOYER	OCCUPATION (SPECIFY)	FROM MONTH	FROM YEAR	TO MONTH	TO YEAR
				PRESENT TIME	

Show below last occupation abroad if not shown above. (Include all information requested above.)

THIS FORM IS SUBMITTED IN CONNECTION WITH APPLICATION FOR: ☐ NATURALIZATION ☐ STATUS AS PERMANENT RESIDENT ☐ OTHER (SPECIFY):	SIGNATURE OF APPLICANT	DATE
Are all copies legible? ☐ Yes	IF YOUR NATIVE ALPHABET IS IN OTHER THAN ROMAN LETTERS WRITE YOUR NAME IN YOUR NATIVE ALPHABET IN THIS SPACE:	

PENALTIES: SEVERE PENALTIES ARE PROVIDED BY LAW FOR KNOWINGLY AND WILLFULLY FALSIFYING OR CONCEALING A MATERIAL FACT.

APPLICANT:
BE SURE TO PUT YOUR NAME AND ALIEN REGISTRATION NUMBER IN THE BOX OUTLINED BY HEAVY BORDER BELOW.

COMPLETE THIS BOX (Family name)	(Given name)	(Middle name)	(Alien registration number)

Form G-325 A (Rev. 10-1-82)   (1) Ident.   101

U.S. Department of Justice
Immigration and Naturalization Service

OMB No. 1115-0136
Employment Eligibility Verification

Please read instructions carefully before completing this form. The instructions must be available during completion of this form. **ANTI-DISCRIMINATION NOTICE.** It is illegal to discriminate against work eligible individuals. Employers **CANNOT** specify which document(s) they will accept from an employee. The refusal to hire an individual because of a future expiration date may also constitute illegal discrimination.

Section 1. Employee Information and Verification. To be completed and signed by employee at the time employment begins

Print Name: Last	First	Middle Initial	Maiden Name
Address (Street Name and Number)		Apt. #	Date of Birth (month/day/year)
City	State	Zip Code	Social Security #

I am aware that federal law provides for imprisonment and/or fines for false statements or use of false documents in connection with the completion of this form.

I attest, under penalty of perjury, that I am (check one of the following):
- ☐ A citizen or national of the United States
- ☐ A Lawful Permanent Resident (Alien # A _____)
- ☐ An alien authorized to work until ____/____/____
  (Alien # or Admission # _____)

Employee's Signature	Date (month/day/year)

Preparer and/or Translator Certification. *(To be completed and signed if Section 1 is prepared by a person other than the employee.) I attest, under penalty of perjury, that I have assisted in the completion of this form and that to the best of my knowledge the information is true and correct.*

Preparer's/Translator's Signature	Print Name
Address (Street Name and Number, City, State, Zip Code)	Date (month/day/year)

Section 2. Employer Review and Verification. To be completed and signed by employer. Examine one document from List A OR examine one document from List B and one from List C as listed on the reverse of this form and record the title, number and expiration date, if any, of the document(s)

List A	OR	List B	AND	List C
Document title:				
Issuing authority:				
Document #:				
Expiration Date (if any): ___/___/___		___/___/___		___/___/___
Document #:				
Expiration Date (if any): ___/___/___				

CERTIFICATION - I attest, under penalty of perjury, that I have examined the document(s) presented by the above-named employee, that the above-listed document(s) appear to be genuine and to relate to the employee named, that the employee began employment on (month/day/year) ____/____/____ and that to the best of my knowledge the employee is eligible to work in the United States. (State employment agencies may omit the date the employee began employment).

Signature of Employer or Authorized Representative	Print Name	Title
Business or Organization Name	Address (Street Name and Number, City, State, Zip Code)	Date (month/day/year)

Section 3. Updating and Reverification. To be completed and signed by employer

A. New Name (if applicable)	B. Date of rehire (month/day/year) (if applicable)

C. If employee's previous grant of work authorization has expired, provide the information below for the document that establishes current employment eligibility.

Document Title: _____ Document #: _____ Expiration Date (if any): ___/___/___

I attest, under penalty of perjury, that to the best of my knowledge, this employee is eligible to work in the United States, and if the employee presented document(s), the document(s) I have examined appear to be genuine and to relate to the individual.

Signature of Employer or Authorized Representative	Date (month/day/year)

Form I-9 (Rev. 11-21-91) N

U.S. Department of Justice
Immigration and Naturalization Service
Please Read Instructions on Page 2

Certificate of Eligibility for Nonimmigrant (F-1) Student Status - For Academic and Language Students

OMB No. 1115-0051

This page must be completed and signed in the U.S. by a designated school official.

1. Family Name (surname)

   First (given) name (do not enter middle name)

   Country of birth

   Date of birth (mo./day/year)

   Country of citizenship

   Admission number (Complete if known)

   For Immigration Official Use

   Visa issuing post | Date Visa issued

   Reinstated, extension granted to:

2. School (school district) name

   School official to be notified of student's arrival in U.S. (Name and Title)

   School address (include zip code)

   School code (including 3-digit suffix, if any) and approval date
   _____ 214F _____ approved on _____

3. This certificate is issued to the student named above for:

   (Check and fill out as appropriate)

   a. ☐ Initial attendance at this school.

   b. ☐ Continued attendance at this school.

   c. ☐ School transfer.

   Transferred from _____.

   d. ☐ Use by dependents for entering the United States.

   e. ☐ Other _____

4. Level of education the student is pursuing or will pursue in the United States

   (check only one)

   a. ☐ Primary   e. ☐ Master's

   b. ☐ Secondary   f. ☐ Doctorate

   c. ☐ Associate   g. ☐ Language training

   d. ☐ Bachelor's   h. ☐ Other

5. The student named above has been accepted for a full course of study at this school, majoring in _____.
   The student is expected to report to the school not later than (date) _____ and complete studies not later than (date) _____
   The normal length of study is _____

6. ☐ English proficiency is required:

   ☐ The student has the required English proficiency.

   ☐ The student is not yet proficient, English instructions will be given at the school.

   ☐ English proficiency is not required because _____

7. This school estimates the student's average costs for an academic term of _____ (up to 12) months to be:

   a. Tuition and fees $ _____

   b. Living expenses $ _____

   c. Expenses of dependents $ _____

   d. Other (specify): $ _____

   Total $ _____

8. This school has information showing the following as the student's means of support, estimated for an academic term of _____ months (Use the same number of months given in item 7).

   a. Student's personal funds $ _____

   b. Funds from this school $ _____
      (specify type)   _____

   c. Funds from another source $ _____
      (specify type and source)   _____

   d. On-campus employment (if any) $ _____

   Total $ _____

9. Remarks: _____
   _____
   _____
   _____
   _____
   _____
   _____

10. School Certification: I certify under penalty of perjury that all information provided above in items 1 through 8 was completed before I signed this form and is true and correct; I executed this form in the United States after review and evaluation in the United States by me or other officials of the school of the student's application, transcripts or other records of courses taken and proof of financial responsibility, which were received at the school prior to the execution of this form; the school has determined that the above named student's qualifications meet all standards for admission to the school; the student will be required to pursue a full course of study as defined by 8 CFR 214.2(f)(6); I am a designated official of the above named school and I am authorized to issue this form.

Signature of designated school official | Name of school official (print or type) | Title | Date issued | Place issued (city and state)

11. Student Certification: I have read and agreed to comply with the terms and conditions of my admission and those of any extension of stay as specified on page 2. I certify that all information provided on this form refers specifically to me and is true and correct to the best of my knowledge. I certify that I seek to enter or remain in the United States temporarily, and solely for the purpose of pursuing a full course of study at the school named on Page 1 of this form. I also authorize the named school to release any information from my records which is needed by the INS pursuant to 8 CFR 214.3(g) to determine my nonimmigrant status.

Signature of student | Name of student | Date

Signature of parent or guardian | Name of parent/guardian (Print or type) | Address(city) | (State or province) | (Country) | (Date)

I-20 SCHOOL

103

IF YOU NEED MORE INFORMATION CONCERNING YOUR F-1 NONIMMIGRANT STUDENT STATUS AND THE RELATING IMMIGRATION PROCEDURES, PLEASE CONTACT EITHER YOUR FOREIGN STUDENT ADVISOR ON CAMPUS OR A NEARBY IMMIGRATION AND NATURALIZATION SERVICE OFFICE.

THIS PAGE, WHEN PROPERLY ENDORSED, MAY BE USED FOR ENTRY OF THE SPOUSE AND CHILDREN OF AN F-1 STUDENT FOLLOWING TO JOIN THE STUDENT IN THE UNITED STATES OR FOR REENTRY OF THE STUDENT TO ATTEND THE SAME SCHOOL AFTER A TEMPORARY ABSENCE FROM THE UNITED STATES.

For reentry of the student and/or the F-2 dependents (EACH CERTIFICATION SIGNATURE IS VALID FOR ONLY ONE YEAR.)

Signature of Designated School Official	Name of School Official (print or type)	Title	Date
Signature of Designated School Official	Name of School Official (print or type)	Title	Date
Signature of Designated School Official	Name of School Official (print or type)	Title	Date
Signature of Designated School Official	Name of School Official (print or type)	Title	Date
Signature of Designated School Official	Name of School Official (print or type)	Title	Date
Signature of Designated School Official	Name of School Official (print or type)	Title	Date

Dependent spouse and children of the F-1 student who are seeking entry/reentry to the U.S.

Name family (caps) first	Date of birth	Country of birth	Relationship to the F-1 student

Student Employment Authorization and other records

| I-94 | IMMIGRATION AND NATURALIZATION SERVICE ARRIVAL/DEPARTURE RECORD | Form Approved OMB No. 1115-077 Expires 8-31-85 |

WELCOME TO THE UNITED STATES

INSTRUCTIONS

- ALL PERSONS EXCEPT U.S. CITIZENS MUST COMPLETE THIS FORM. A SEPARATE FORM MUST BE COMPLETED FOR EACH PERSON IN YOUR GROUP.

- TYPE OR PRINT LEGIBLY WITH PEN IN ALL CAPITAL LETTERS. USE ENGLISH. DO NOT WRITE ON THE BACK OF THIS FORM.

- This form is in two parts, an ARRIVAL RECORD (Items 1 through 7), and a DEPARTURE RECORD (Items 8 through 10). *You must complete both parts.* Enter exactly the same information in spaces 8, 9, and 10 as you enter in spaces 1, 2, and 3.

  * *Item 7.* If you entered the United States by land, enter "LAND" in this space.

- WHEN YOU HAVE COMPLETED ALL REQUIRED ITEMS, PRESENT THIS FORM TO THE U.S. IMMIGRATION AND NATURALIZATION INSPECTOR.

ADMISSION NUMBER

996-00450273

I-94 ARRIVAL RECORD
(Rev. 1-1-83)N

1. FAMILY NAME (SURNAME) *(leave one space between names)*

FIRST (GIVEN) NAME *(do not enter middle name)*

2. DATE OF BIRTH

DAY | MO. | YR.

3. COUNTRY OF CITIZENSHIP

4. COUNTRY OF RESIDENCE *(country where you live)*

5. ADDRESS WHILE IN THE UNITED STATES *(Number and Street)*

City

State

CITY WHERE USA WAS ISSUED

AIRLINE & FLIGHT NO. OR SHIP NAME*

THIS FORM IS REQUIRED BY THE IMMIGRATION AND NATURALIZATION SERVICE, UNITED STATES DEPARTMENT OF JUSTICE.

SAMPLE

WARNING
- A nonimmigrant who accepts unauthorized employment is subject to deportation.

IMPORTANT
- Retain this permit in your possession; you must surrender it when you leave the U.S. Failure to do so may delay your entry into the U.S. in the future.

ADMISSION NUMBER

996-00450273

8. FAMILY NAME (SURNAME) *(same as Family Name in Item 1 above)*

FIRST (GIVEN) NAME *(same as First Name in Item 1 above)*

9. DATE OF BIRTH *(same as Item 2)*

DAY | MO. | YR.

10. COUNTRY OF CITIZENSHIP *(same as Item 3 above)*

SEE REVERSE SIDE FOR OTHER IMPORTANT INFORMATION

| U.S. IMMIGRATION AND NATURALIZATION SERVICE | I-94 DEPARTURE RECORD (Rev. 1-1-83)N |

START HERE - Please Type or Print

Part 1. Information about the employer filing this petition.

If the employer is an individual, use the top name line. Organizations should use the second line.

Family Name	Given Name	Middle Initial

Company or Organization Name

Address - Attn:

Street Number and Name		Apt. #
City	State or Province	
Country	ZIP/Postal Code	

IRS Tax #

Part 2. Information about this Petition.

(See instructions to determine the fee).

1. **Requested Nonimmigrant Classification:**
   (write classification symbol at right) _____

2. **Basis for Classification** (check one)
   a. ☐ New employment
   b. ☐ Continuation of previously approved employment without change
   c. ☐ Change in previously approved employment
   d. ☐ New concurrent employment

3. **Prior petition.** If you checked other than "New Employment" in item 2 (above) give the most recent prior petition number for the worker(s):

4. **Requested Action:** (check one)
   a. ☐ Notify the office in Part 4 so the person(s) can obtain a visa or be admitted (NOTE: a petition is not required for an E-1, E-2, or R visa).
   b. ☐ Change the person(s) status and extend their stay since they are all now in the U.S. in another status (see instructions for limitations). This is available only where you check "New Employment" in item 2, above.
   c. ☐ Extend or amend the stay of the person(s) since they now hold this status.

5. **Total number of workers in petition:** _____

(See instructions for where more than one worker can be included.)

Part 3. Information about the person(s) you are filing for.

Complete the blocks below. Use the continuation sheet to name each person included in this petition.

If an entertainment group, give their group name.

Family Name	Given Name	Middle Initial
Date of Birth (Month/Day/Year)	Country of Birth	
Social Security #	A #	

If In the United States, complete the following:

Date of Arrival (Month/Day/Year)	I-94 #
Current Nonimmigrant Status	Expires (Month/Day/Year)

FOR INS USE ONLY

Returned	Receipt
Resubmitted	
Reloc Sent	
Reloc Rec'd	

Interviewed
☐ Petitioner
☐ Beneficiary

Class: _____
# of Workers: _____
Priority Number: _____
Validity Dates: From _____
                    To _____

☐ **Classification Approved**
   ☐ Consulate/POE/PFI Notified

   At: _____
   ☐ Extension Granted
   ☐ COS/Extension Granted

Partial Approval (explain)

Action Block

To Be Completed by Attorney or Representative, if any
☐ Fill in box if G-28 is attached to represent the applicant
VOLAG#

ATTY State License #

106

Part 4.   Processing Information.

If the person named in Part 3 is outside the U.S. or a requested extension of stay or change of status cannot be granted, give the U.S. consulate or inspection facility you want notified if this petition is approved.

Type of Office (check one): ☐ Consulate	☐ Pre-flight inspection	☐ Port of Entry
Office Address (City)		U.S. State or Foreign Country

Person's Foreign Address

Does each person in this petition have a valid passport?		
☐ Not required to have passport	☐ No - explain on separate paper	☐ Yes
Are you filing any other petitions with this one?	☐ No	☐ Yes - How many? _____
Are applications for replacement/Initial I-94's being filed with this petition?	☐ No	☐ Yes - How many? _____
Are applications by dependents being filed with this petition?	☐ No	☐ Yes - How many? _____
Is any person in this petition in exclusion or deportation proceedings?	☐ No	☐ Yes - explain on separate paper
Have you ever filed an immigrant petition for any person in this petition?	☐ No	☐ Yes - explain on separate paper

If you indicated you were filing a new petition in Part 2, within the past 7 years has any person in this petition:

1) ever been given the classification you are now requesting?	☐ No	☐ Yes - explain on separate paper
2) ever been denied the classification you are now requesting?	☐ No	☐ Yes - explain on separate paper

If you are filing for an entertainment group, has any person in this petition not been with the group for at least 1 year?

☐ No   ☐ Yes - explain on separate paper.

Part 5.   Basic Information about the proposed employment and employer.
Attach the supplement relating to the classification you are requesting.

	Nontechnical Description of Job

Address where the person(s) will work if different from the address in Part 1.

Is this a full-time position?		Wages per week or per year
☐ No - Hours per week	☐ Yes	

Other Compensation (explain)	Value per week or per year	Dates of Intended employment From: To:

Type of Petitioner - check one: ☐ U.S. citizen or permanent resident	☐ Organization	☐ Other - explain on separate paper
Type of Business:		Year established:
Current Number of Employees	Gross Annual Income	Net Annual Income

Part 6.   Signature.
Read the information on penalties in the instructions before completing this section.

I certify, under penalty of perjury under the laws of the United States of America, that this petition, and the evidence submitted with it, is all true and correct. If filing this on behalf of an organization, I certify that I am empowered to do so by that organization, If this petition is to extend a prior petition I certify that the proposed employment is under the same terms and conditions as in the prior approved petition, I authorize the release of any information from my records,or from the petitioning organization's records, which the Immigration and Naturalization Service needs to determine eligibility for the benefit being sought.

Signature and title	Print Name	Date

Please Note: If you do not completely fill out this form and the required supplement, or fail to submit required documents listed in the instructions, then the person(s) filed for may not be found eligible for the requested benefit, and this petition may be denied.

Part 7.   Signature of person preparing form if other than above.

I declare that I prepared this petition at the request of the above person and it is based on all information of which I have any knowledge.

Signature	Print Name	Date

Firm Name
and Address

Supplement-1

Attach to Form I-129 when more than one person is included in the petition. *(List each person separately. Do n̄* *include the person you named on the form).*

Family Name	Given Name	Middle Initial	Date of Birth (month/day/year)
Country of Birth	Social Security No.	A#	

IF	Date of Arrival (month/day/year)	I-94#	
IN THE	Current Nonimmigrant Status	Expires on (month/day/year)	
U.S.			

Country where passport issued	Expiration Date (month/day/year)	Date Started with group

Family Name	Given Name	Middle Initial	Date of Birth (month/day/year)
Country of Birth	Social Security No.	A#	

IF	Date of Arrival (month/day/year)	I-94#	
IN THE	Current Nonimmigrant Status:	Expires on (month/day/year)	
U.S.			

Country where passport issued	Expiration Date (month/day/year)	Date Started with group

Family Name	Given Name	Middle Initial	Date of Birth (month/day/year)
Country of Birth	Social Security No.	A#	

IF	Date of Arrival (month/day/year)	I-94#	
IN THE	Current Nonimmigrant Status:	Expires on (month/day/year)	
U.S.			

Country where passport issued	Expiration Date (month/day/year)	Date Started with group

Family Name	Given Name	Middle Initial	Date of Birth (month/day/year)
Country of Birth	Social Security No.	A#	

IF	Date of Arrival (month/day/year)	I-94#	
IN THE	Current Nonimmigrant Status:	Expires on (month/day/year)	
U.S.			

Country where passport issued	Expiration Date (month/day/year)	Date Started with group

Family Name	Given Name	Middle Initial	Date of Birth (month/day/year)
Country of Birth	Social Security No.	A#	

IF	Date of Arrival (month/day/year)	I-94#	
IN THE	Current Nonimmigrant Status:	Expires on (month/day/year)	
U.S.			

Country where passport issued	Expiration Date (month/day/year)	Date Started with group

108

U.S. Department of Justice

Immigration and Naturalization Service

H Classification

Supplement to Form I-129

Name of person or organization filing petition:

Name of person or total number of workers or trainees you are filing for:

List the alien's and any dependent family members; prior periods of stay in H classification in the U.S. for the last six years. Be sure to list only those periods in which the alien and/or family members were actually in the U.S. in an H classification. If more space is needed, attach an additional sheet.

Classification sought (check one):

- [ ] H-1A — Registered Professional nurse
- [ ] H-1B1 — Specialty occupation
- [ ] H-1B2 — Exceptional services relating to a cooperative research and development project administered by the U.S. Department of Defense
- [ ] H-1B3 — Artist, entertainer or fashion model of national or international acclaim

- [ ] H-1B4 — Artist or entertainer in unique or traditional art form
- [ ] H-1B5 — Athlete
- [ ] H-1BS — Essential Support Personnel for H-1B entertainer or athlete
- [ ] H-2A — Agricultural worker
- [ ] H-2B — Nonagricultural worker
- [ ] H-3 — Trainee
- [ ] H-3 — Special education exchange visitor program

Section 1. Complete this section if filing for H-1A or H-1B classification.

Describe the proposed duties.

Alien's present occupation and summary of prior work experience.

Statement for H-1B specialty occupations only:

By filing this petition, I agree to the terms of the labor condition application for the duration of the alien's authorized period of stay for H-1B employment.

Petitioner's Signature   Date

Statement for H-1B specialty occupations and DOD projects:

As an authorized official of the employer, I certify that the employer will be liable for the reasonable costs of return transportation of the alien abroad if the alien is dismissed from employment by the employer before the end of the period of authorized stay.

Signature of authorized official of employer   Date

Statement for H-1B DOD projects only:

I certify that the alien will be working on a cooperative research and development project or a coproduction project under a reciprocal Government-to-Government agreement administered by the Department of Defense.

DOD project manager's signature   Date

Section 2. Complete this section if filing for H-2A or H-2B classification.

Employment is:
(check one)
- [ ] Seasonal
- [ ] Peakload
- [ ] Intermittent
- [ ] One-time occurrence

Temporary need is:
(check one)
- [ ] Unpredictable
- [ ] Periodic
- [ ] Recurrent annually

Explain your temporary need for the alien's services (attach a separate paper if additional space is needed).

Section 3. Complete this section if filing for H-2A classification.

The petitioner and each employer consent to allow government access to the site where the labor is being performed for the purpose of determining compliance with H-2A requirements. The petitioner further agrees to notify the Service in the manner and within the time frame specified if an H-2A worker absconds or if the authorized employment ends more than five days before the relating certification document expires, and pay liquidated damages of dollars for each instance where it cannot demonstrate compliance with this notification requirement. The petitioner also agrees to pay liquidated damages two hundred dollars for each instance where it cannot be demonstrated that the H-2A worker either departed the United States or obtained authorized sta during the period of admission or within five days of early termination, whichever comes first.

The petitioner must execute Part A. If the petitioner is the employer's agent, the employer must execute Part B. If there are joint employers, they must ea execute Part C.

Part A. Petitioner:

By filing this petition, I agree to the conditions of H-2A employment, and agree to the notice requirements and limited liabilities defined in CFR 214.2 (h) (3) (vi).

Petitioner's signature   Date

Part B. Employer who is not petitioner:

I certify that I have authorized the party filing this petition to act as my agent in this regard. I assume full responsibi for all representations made by this agent on my behalf, and agree to the conditions of H-2A eligibility.

Employer's signature   Date

Part C. Joint Employers:

I agree to the conditions of H-2A eligibility.

Joint employer's signature(s)   Date

Joint employer's signature(s)   Date

Joint employer's signature(s)   Date

Joint employer's signature(s)   Date

Joint employer's signature(s)   Date

Section 4. Complete this section if filing for H-3 classification.

If you answer "yes" to any of the following questions, attach a full explanation.

a.	Is the training you intend to provide, or similar training, available in the alien's country?	☐ No	☐ Yes
b.	Will the training benefit the alien in pursuing a career abroad?	☐ No	☐ Yes
c.	Does the training involve productive employment incidental to training?	☐ No	☐ Yes
d.	Does the alien already have skills related to the training?	☐ No	☐ Yes
e.	Is this training an effort to overcome a labor shortage?	☐ No	☐ Yes
f.	Do you intend to employ the alien abroad at the end of this training?	☐ No	☐ Yes

If you do not intend to employ this person abroad at the end of this training, explain why you wish to incur the cost of providing this training, a your expected return from this training.

U.S. Department of Justice
Immigration and Naturalization Service

E Classification
Supplement to Form I-129

Name of person or organization filing petition:	Name of person you are filing for:

Classification sought (check one):	Name of country signatory to treaty with U.S.
☐ E-1 Treaty trader ☐ E-2 Treaty investor	

Section 1.   **Information about the Employer Outside the U.S. (if any)**

Name	Address
Alien's Position - Title, duties and number of years employed	Principal Product, merchandise or service
Total Number of Employees	

Section 2.   **Additional Information about the U.S. Employer.**

The U.S. company is, to the company outside the U.S. (check one):
☐ Parent   ☐ Branch   ☐ Subsidiary   ☐ Affiliate   ☐ Joint Venture

Date and Place of Incorporation or establishment in the U.S.

Nationality of Ownership (Individual or Corporate)

Name	Nationality	Immigration Status	% Ownership

Assets	Net Worth	Total Annual Income

Staff in the U.S.	Executive/Manager	Specialized Qualifications or Knowledge
Nationals of Treaty Country in E or L Status	_____	_____
Total number of employees in the U.S.	_____	_____

Total number of employees the alien would supervise; or describe the nature of the specialized skills essential to the U.S. company.

Section 3.   **Complete if filing for an E-1 Treaty Trader**

Total Annual Gross Trade/Business of the U.S. company $	For Year Ending

Percent of total gross trade which is between the U.S. and the country of which the treaty trader organization is a national.

Section 4.   **Complete if filing for an E-2 Treaty Investor**

Total Investment:	Cash $	Equipment $	Other $
	Inventory $	Premises $	Total $

Name of person or organization filing petition: | Name of person you are filing for:

This petition is (check one): ☐ An individual petition ☐ A blanket petition

Section 1. Complete this section if filing an individual petition.

Classification sought (check one): ☐ L-1A manager or executive ☐ L-1B specialized knowledge

List the alien's, and any dependent family members' prior periods of stay in an L classification in the U.S. for the last seven years. Be sure to list o those periods in which the alien and/or family members were actually in the U.S. in an L classification.

Name and address of employer abroad

Dates of alien's employment with this employer. Explain any interruptions in employment.

Description of the alien's duties for the past 3 years.

Description of alien's proposed duties in the U.S.

Summarize the alien's education and work experience.

The U.S. company is, to the company abroad: (check one)
☐ Parent ☐ Branch ☐ Subsidiary ☐ Affiliate ☐ Joint Venture
Describe the stock ownership and managerial control of each company.

Do the companies currently have the same qualifying relationship as they did during the one-year period of the alien's employment with the compa abroad? ☐ Yes ☐ No (attach explanation)

Is the alien coming to the U.S. to open a new office?
☐ Yes (explain in detail on separate paper) ☐ No

Section 2. Complete this section if filing a Blanket Petition.

List all U.S. and foreign parent, branches, subsidiaries and affiliates included in this petition. (Attach a separate paper if additional space is neede
Name and Address   Relationship

Explain in detail on separate paper.

Form I-129 Supplement E/L (12/11/91) N

O and P Classifications
Supplement to Form I-129

S. Department of Justice
migration and Naturalization Service

me of person or organization filing petition:

Name of person or group or total number of workers you are filing for:

assification sought (check one):

☐ **O-1** Alien of extraordinary ability in sciences, art, education, or business.

☐ **P-2** Artist or entertainer for reciprocal exchange program

☐ **P-2S** Essential Support Personnel for **P-2**

plain the nature of the event

scribe the duties to be performed

filing for O-2 or P support alien, dates of the alien's prior experience with the O-1 or P alien

ave you obtained the required written consultations(s)?   ☐ Yes - attached   ☐ No - Copy of request attached
not, give the following information about the organizations(s) to which you have sent a duplicate of this petition.

O-1 Extraordinary ability

Name of recognized peer group | Phone #

Address | Date sent

O-1 Extraordinary achievement in motion pictures or television

Name of labor organization | Phone #

Address | Date sent

Name of management organization | Phone #

Address | Date sent

O-2 or P alien

Name of labor organization | Phone #

Address | Date sent

Form I-129 Supplement O/P/Q/R (12/11/91) N

Name of person or organization filing petition:

Name of person you are filing for:

Section 1.   Complete this section if you are filing for a Q international cultural exchange alien.

I hereby certify that the participant(s) in this international cultural exchange program:
- is at least 18 years of age,
- has the ability to communicate effectively about the cultural attributes of his or her country of nationality to the American public, and
- has not previously been in the United States as a Q nonimmigrant unless he/she has resided and been physically present outside the U.S. the immediate prior year.

I also certify that the same wages and working conditions are accorded the participants as are provided to similarly employed U.S. workers.

Petitioner's signature

Date

Section 2.   Complete this section if you are filing for an R religious worker.

List the alien's, and any dependent family members, prior periods of stay in R classification in the U.S. for the last six years, Be sure to list only th periods in which the alien and/or family members were actually in the U.S. in an R classification.

Describe the alien's proposed duties in the U.S.

Describe the alien's qualifications for the vocation or occupation

Description of the relationship between the U.S. religious organization and the organization abroad of which the alien was a member.

START HERE - Please Type or Print

Part 1.   Information about employer.

Sponsoring Company or Organization's Name

Address - ATTN:

Street Number and Name		Room #
City or Town	State or Province	
Country		ZIP/Postal Code

Part 2.   Information about employment.

This alien will be a:

a. ☐   manager/executive

b. ☐   specialized knowledge professional

Blanket petition approval number is: _____

Part 3.   Information about employee.

Family Name	Given Name	Middle Initial

Foreign Address
Street Number and Name / Apt. #

City	State or Province	
Country		ZIP/Postal Code

Date of Birth (Month/Day/Year) / Country of Birth

Part 4.   Additional information about the employment.

Address

Street Number and Name		Room #
City or Town	State or Province	
Country		ZIP/Postal Code

Dates of intended employment (Month/Day/Year)   From ___   To ___

Weekly Wage	Hours per Week

Title and detailed description of duties to be performed.

FOR INS USE ONLY

Returned	Receipt
_____	
_____	

Resubmitted

_____

_____

Reloc Sent

_____

_____

Reloc Rec'd

☐ Petitioner Interviewed
☐ Beneficiary Interviewed

Approved as:
☐   manager/executive
☐   specialized knowledge professional

Validity dates
From: _____

To: _____

Denied (give reason)

Action Block

To Be Completed by Attorney or Representative, If any

☐   Fill in box if G-28 is attached to represent the petitioner

VOLAG#

ATTY State License #

115

Form I-129S (Rev. 12/20/91) N

Part 4. (Continued).

Give the aliens dates of prior periods of stay in the U.S. in a worked authorized capacity and the type of visa.

_____

_____

_____

_____

Give the alien's dates of employment and job duties for the immediate prior three years.

_____

_____

_____

_____

Summarize the alien's education and other work experience.

_____

_____

_____

_____

_____

_____

Part 5. Signature. Read the information on penalties in the instructions before completing this section.

I certify, under penalty of perjury under the laws of the United States of America, that this petition, and the evidence submitted with it, is all true and correct filing this on behalf of an organization, I certify that I am empowered to do so by that organization. If this petition is to extend a prior petition, I certify that proposed employment is under the same terms and conditions as in the prior approved petition. I authorize the release of any information from my records from the petitioning organization's records, which the Immigration and Naturalization Service needs to determine eligibility for the benefit being sought.

Signature   Print Name   Date

Please Note: If you do not completely fill out this form, or fail to submit required documents listed in the instructions, then the person(s) filed for cannot be f eligible for the requested benefit, and your petition may be denied.

Part 6. Signature of person preparing form if other than above.

I declare that I prepared this application at the request of the above person and it is based on all information of which I have knowledge.

Signature   Print Name   Date

Firm Name
and Address

*U.S. Government Printing Office: 1992 — 312-328/5

S. Department of Justice
Immigration and Naturalization Service (INS)

OMB #1115-0054
Petition for Alien Relative

DO NOT WRITE IN THIS BLOCK - FOR EXAMINING OFFICE ONLY

Case ID#	Action Stamp	Fee Stamp
A#		
G-28 or Volag #		

Section of Law:
- [ ] 201 (b) spouse
- [ ] 201 (b) child
- [ ] 201 (b) parent
- [ ] 203 (a)(1)
- [ ] 203 (a)(2)
- [ ] 203 (a)(4)
- [ ] 203 (a)(5)

AM CON: _____

Petition was filed on: _____ (priority date)
- [ ] Personal Interview
- [ ] Pet. [ ] Ben. "A" File Reviewed
- [ ] Field Investigations
- [ ] 204 (a)(2)(A) Resolved
- [ ] Previously Forwarded
- [ ] Stateside Criteria
- [ ] I-485 Simultaneously
- [ ] 204 (h) Resolved

Remarks:

Relationship

The alien relative is my:
- [ ] Husband/Wife
- [ ] Parent
- [ ] Brother/Sister
- [ ] Child

2. Are you related by adoption?
- [ ] Yes
- [ ] No

3. Did you gain permanent residence through adoption?
- [ ] Yes
- [ ] No

Information about you

Name (Family name in CAPS) (First) (Middle)

Address (Number and Street) (Apartment Number)

(Town or City) (State/Country) (ZIP/Postal Code)

Place of Birth (Town or City) (State/Country)

Date of Birth (Mo/Day/Yr)

5. **Sex**
- [ ] Male
- [ ] Female

6. **Marital Status**
- [ ] Married
- [ ] Single
- [ ] Widowed
- [ ] Divorced

Other Names Used (including maiden name)

Date and Place of Present Marriage (if married)

Social Security Number

10. **Alien Registration Number** (if any)

Names of Prior Husbands/Wives 12. **Date(s) Marriage(s) Ended**

If you are a U.S. citizen, complete the following:
My citizenship was acquired through (check one)
- [ ] Birth in the U.S.
- [ ] Naturalization(Give number of certificate,date and place it was issued)

- [ ] Parents
   Have you obtained a certificate of citizenship in your own name?
   - [ ] Yes
   - [ ] No
   If "Yes", give number of certificate, date and place it was issued

If you are a lawful permanent resident alien, complete the following:
Date and place of admission for, or adjustment to, lawful permanent residence and class of admission:

Did you gain permanent resident status through marriage to a United States citizen or lawful permanent resident? [ ] Yes [ ] No

C. Information about your alien relative

1. **Name** (Family name in CAPS) (First) (Middle)

2. **Address** (Number and Street) (Apartment Number)

(Town or City) (State/Country) (ZIP/Postal Code)

Place of Birth (Town or City) (State/Country)

Date of Birth (Mo/Day/Yr)

5. **Sex**
- [ ] Male
- [ ] Female

6. **Marital Status**
- [ ] Married
- [ ] Single
- [ ] Widowed
- [ ] Divorced

7. **Other Names Used** (including maiden name)

8. **Date and Place of Present Marriage** (if married)

9. **Social Security Number**

10. **Alien Registration Number** (if any)

11. **Names of Prior Husbands/Wives** 12. **Dates(s) Marriage(s) Ended**

13. Has your relative ever been in the U.S.?
- [ ] Yes
- [ ] No

14. If your relative is currently in the U.S., complete the following: He or she last arrived as a (visitor, student, stowaway, without inspection, etc.)

Arrival/Departure Record (I-94) Number   Date arrived (Month/Day/Year)

Date authorized stay expired, or will expire as shown on Form I-94 or I-95

15. Name and address of present employer (if any)

Date this employment began (Month/Day/Year)

16. Has your relative ever been under immigration proceedings?
- [ ] Yes
- [ ] No   Where _____ When _____
- [ ] Exclusion [ ] Deportation [ ] Rescission [ ] Judicial Proceedings

INITIAL RECEIPT	RESUBMITTED	RELOCATED		COMPLETED		
		Rec'd	Sent	Approved	Denied	Returned

Form I-130 (Rev. 4/11/91) Y

C. (continued) Information about your alien relative

16. List husbands/wife and all children of your relative (if your relative is your husband/wife, list only his or her children).

(Name)	(Relationship)	(Date of Birth)	(Country of Birth)

17. Address in the United States where your relative intends to live

(Number and Street)	(Town or City)	(State)

18. Your relative's address abroad

(Number and Street)	(Town or City)	(Province)	(Country)	(Phone Number)

19. If your relative's native alphabet is other than Roman letters, write his/her name and address abroad in the native alphabet:

(Name)	(Number and Street)	(Town or City)	(Province)	(Country)

20. If filing for your husband/wife, give last address at which you both lived together: From / To

(Name)	(Number and Street)	(Town or City)	(Province)	(Country)	(Month)	(Year)	(Month)	(Year)

21. Check the appropriate box below and give the information required for the box you checked:

☐ Your relative will apply for a visa abroad at the American Consulate in _____
(City) _____ (Country)

☐ Your relative is in the United States and will apply for adjustment of status to that of a lawful permanent resident in the office of the Immigration and Naturalization Service at _____
(City) _____ (State) . If your relative is not eligible for adjustment of status, he or she will

apply for a visa abroad at the American Consulate in _____
(City) _____ (Country)

(Designation of a consulate outside the country of your relative's last residence does not guarantee acceptance for processing by that consulate. Acceptance is at the discretion of the designated consulate.)

D. Other Information

1. If separate petitions are also being submitted for other relatives, give names of each and relationship.

2. Have you ever filed a petition for this or any other alien before? ☐ Yes ☐ No
   If "Yes," give name, place and date of filing, and result.

Warning: The INS investigates claimed relationships and verifies the validity of documents. The INS seeks criminal prosecutions when family relationships are falsified to obtain visas.

Penalties: You may, by law be imprisoned for not more than five years, or fined $250,000, or both, for entering into a marriage contract for the purpose of evading any provision of the immigration laws and you may be fined up to $10,000 or imprisoned up to five years or both, for knowingly and willfully falsifying or concealing a material fact or using any false document in submitting this petition.

Your Certification: I certify, under penalty of perjury under the laws of the United States of America, that the foregoing is true and correct. Furthermore, I authorize the release of any information from my records which the Immigration and Naturalization Service needs to determine eligibility for the benefit that I am seeking.

Signature _____ Date _____ Phone Number _____

Signature of Person Preparing Form if Other than Above

I declare that I prepared this document at the request of the person above and that it is based on all information of which I have any knowledge.

Print Name _____ (Address) _____ (Signature) _____ (Date) _____

G-28 ID Number _____

118

Volag Number _____

NOTICE TO PERSONS FILING FOR SPOUSES IF MARRIED LESS THAN TWO YEARS

Pursuant to section 216 of the Immigration and Nationality Act, your alien spouse may be granted conditional permanent resident status in the United States as of the date he or she is admitted or adjusted to conditional status by an officer of the Immigration and Naturalization Service. Both you and your conditional permanent resident spouse are required to file a petition, Form I-751, Joint Petition to Remove Conditional Basis of Alien's Permanent Resident Status, during the ninety day period immediately before the second anniversary of the date your alien spouse was granted conditional permanent residence.

Otherwise, the rights, privileges, responsibilities and duties which apply to all other permanent residents apply equally to a conditional permanent resident. A conditional permanent resident is not limited to the right to apply for naturalization, to file petitions in behalf of qualifying relatives, or to reside permanently in the United States as an immigrant in accordance with the immigration laws.

> **Failure to file Form I-751, Joint Petition to Remove the Conditional Basis of Alien's Permanent Resident Status, will result in termination of permanent residence status and initiation of deportation proceedings.**

NOTE: You must complete Items 1 through 6 to assure that petition approval is recorded. Do not write in the section below item 6.

Name of relative (Family name in CAPS)   (First)   (Middle)

Other names used by relative (Including maiden name)

Country of relative's birth   4.   Date of relative's birth (Month/Day/Year)

Your name (Last name in CAPS)   (First)   (Middle)   6.   Your phone number

n Stamp

SECTION	DATE PETITION FILED
☐ 201 (b)(spouse)	
☐ 201 (b)(child)	
☐ 201 (b)(parent)	
☐ 203 (a)(1)	☐ STATESIDE
☐ 203 (a)(2)	CRITERIA GRANTED
☐ 203 (a)(4)	
☐ 203 (a)(5)	SENT TO CONSUL AT;

CHECKLIST

Have you answered each question?
Have you signed the petition?
Have you enclosed:

- ☐ The filing fee for each petition?
- ☐ Proof of your citizenship or lawful permanent residence?
- ☐ All required supporting documents for each petition?

If you are filing for your husband or wife have you included:

- ☐ Your picture?
- ☐ His or her picture?
- ☐ Your G-325A?
- ☐ His or her G-325A?

119

ive Petition Card
I-130A (Rev. 4/11/91) Y

U.S. Department of Justice
Immigration and Naturalization Service

OMB #1115-0005
Application for Travel Document

START HERE - Please Type or Print

Part 1.   Information about you.

Family Name	Given Name	Middle Initial

Address - C/O

Street Number and Name		Apt. #
City	State or Province	
Country		ZIP/Postal Code

Date of Birth (month/day/year)	Country of Birth
Social Security #	A #

Part 2.   Application Type (check one).

a. ☐ I am a permanent resident or conditional resident of the United States and I am applying for a Reentry Permit.

b. ☐ I now hold U.S. refugee or asylee status and I am applying for a Refugee Travel Document.

c. ☐ I am a permanent resident as a direct result of refugee or asylee status, and am applying for a Refugee Travel Document.

d. ☐ I am applying for an Advance Parole to allow me to return to the U.S. after temporary foreign travel.

e. ☐ I am outside the U.S. and am applying for an Advance Parole.

f. ☐ I am applying for an Advance Parole for another person who is outside the U.S. *Give the following information about that person:*

Family Name	Given Name	Middle Initial
Date of Birth (Month/Day/Year)	Country of Birth	

Foreign Address - C/O

Street Number and Name		Apt. #
City	State or Province	
Country		ZIP/Postal Code

Part 3.   Processing Information.

Date of Intended departure (Month/Day/Year)	Expected length of trip.

Are you, or any person included in this application, now in exclusion or deportation proceedings?
☐ No   ☐ Yes, at (give office name) _____

If applying for an Advance Parole Document, skip to Part 7.

Have you ever before been issued a Reentry Permit or Refugee Travel Document?
☐ No   ☐ Yes (give the following for the last document issued to you)

Date Issued	Disposition (attached, lost, etc.)

Form I-131 (Rev. 12/10/91) N

Continued on back.

FOR INS USE ONLY

Returned	Receipt

_____

_____

Resubmitted

_____

_____

Reloc Sent

_____

_____

Reloc Rec'd

☐ Applicant Interviewed on

Document Issued
☐ Reentry Permit
☐ Refugee Travel Document
☐ Single Advance Parole
☐ Multiple Advance Parole
Validity to _____

If Reentry Permit or Refugee Travel Document
☐ Mail to Address in Part 2
☐ Mail to American Consulate
☐ Mail to INS overseas office
AT

Remarks:
☐ Document Hand Delivered
On   By

Action Block

To Be Completed by *Attorney* or *Representative*, if any
☐ Fill in box if G-28 is attached to represent the applicant

VOLAG#

ATTY State License #

Part 3. Processing Information. (continued)

Where do you want this travel document sent? (check one)

- ☐ Address in Part 2, above
- ☐ American Consulate at (give City and Country, below)
- ☐ INS overseas office at (give City and Country, below)

City   Country

If you checked b. or c., above, give your overseas address:

Part 4. Information about the Proposed Travel.

Purpose of trip. *If you need more room, continue on a separate sheet of paper.*	List the countries you intend to visit.

Part 5. Complete only if applying for a Reentry Permit.

Since becoming a Permanent Resident (or during the past five years, whichever is less) how much total time have you spent outside the United States?	☐ less than 6 months ☐ 2 to 3 years ☐ 6 months to 1 year ☐ 3 to 4 years ☐ 1 to 2 years ☐ more than 4 years
Since you became a Permanent Resident, have you ever filed a federal income tax return as a nonresident, or failed to file a federal return because you considered yourself to be a nonresident? (if yes, give details on a separate sheet of paper).	☐ Yes ☐ No

Part 6. Complete only if applying for a Refugee Travel Document.

Country from which you are a refugee or asylee:

If you answer yes to any of the following questions, explain on a separate sheet of paper.

Do you plan to travel to the above-named country?	☐ Yes ☐ No
Since you were accorded Refugee/Asylee status, have you ever: returned to the above-named country; applied for an/or obtained a national passport, passport renewal, or entry permit into this country; or applied for an/or received any benefit from such country, (for example, health insurance benefits?)	☐ Yes ☐ No
Since being accorded Refugee/Asylee status, have you, by any legal procedure or voluntary act, re-acquired the nationality of the above-named country, acquired a new nationality, or been granted refugee or asylee status in any other country?	☐ Yes ☐ No

Part 7. Complete only if applying for an Advance Parole.

On a separate sheet of paper, please explain how you qualify for an Advance Parole and what circumstances warrant issuance of Advance Parole. Include copies of any documents you wish considered. (See instructions.)

For how may trips do you intend to use this document?   ☐ 1 trip   ☐ More than 1 trip

If outside the U.S., at right give the U.S. Consulate or INS office you wish notified if this application is approved.

Part 8. Signature. Read the information on penalties in the instructions before completing this section. You must file this application while in the United States if filing for a reentry permit or refugee travel document.

I certify under penalty of perjury under the laws of the United States of America that this petition, and the evidence submitted with it, is all true and correct. I authorize the release of any information from my records which the Immigration and Naturalization Service needs to determine eligibility for the benefit I am seeking.

Signature   Date   Daytime Telephone #
(   )

Please Note: *If you do not completely fill out this form, or fail to submit required documents listed in the instructions, you may not be found eligible for the requested document and this application will have to be denied.*

Part 9. Signature of person preparing form if other than above. (sign below)

I declare that I prepared this application at the request of the above person and it is based on all information of which I have knowledge.

Signature   Print Your Name   Date

Firm Name   Daytime Telephone #
and Address   (   )

* U.S. GPO: 1992-312-328/51145

U.S. Department of Justice
Immigration and Naturalization Service

OMB #1115-0214

Affidavit of Support Under Section 213A of the Act

START HERE - Please Type or Print

Part 1. Information on Sponsor (You)

Last Name	First Name	Middle Name

Mailing Address *(Street Number and Name)*	Apt/Suite Number

City	State or Province

Country	ZIP/Postal Code	Telephone Number ( )

Place of Residence if different from above *(Street Number and Name)*	Apt/Suite Number

City	State or Province

Country	ZIP/Postal Code	Telephone Number ( )

Date of Birth *(Month, Day, Year)*	Place of Birth *(City, State, Country)*	Are you a U.S. Citizen? Yes No

Social Security Number	A-Number *(If any)*

FOR AGENCY USE ONLY

This Affidavit   Receipt

[ ] Meets

[ ] Does not meet

Requirements of Section 213A

Officer's Signature

Location

Date

Part 2. Basis for Filing Affidavit of Support

I am filing this affidavit of support because *(check one):*

a.   I filed/am filing the alien relative petition.

b.   I filed/am filing an alien worker petition on behalf of the intending immigrant, who is related to me as my _____ *(relationship)*

c.   I have ownership interest of at least 5% of _____ *(name of entity which filed visa petition)*, which filed an alien worker petition on behalf of the intending immigrant, who is related to me as my _____ *(relationship)*

d.   I am a joint sponsor willing to accept the legal obligations with any other sponsor(s).

Part 3. Information on the Immigrant(s) You Are Sponsoring

Last Name	First Name	Middle Name

Date of Birth *(Month, Day, Year)*	Sex: Male Female	Social Security Number *(If any)*

Country of Citizenship	A-Number *(If any)*

Current Address *(Street Number and Name)*	Apt/Suite Number	City

State/Province	Country	ZIP/Postal Code	Telephone Number ( )

List any spouse and/or children immigrating with the immigrant named above in this Part: *(Use additional sheet of paper if necessary.)*

Name	Relationship to Sponsored Immigrant			Date of Birth			A-Number *(If any)*	Social Security Number *(If any)*
	Spouse	Son	Daughter	Mo.	Day	Yr.		

Form I-864 (10/6/97)

Part 4. Eligibility to Sponsor

To be a sponsor you must be a U.S. citizen or national or a lawful permanent resident. If you are not the petitioning relative, you must provide proof of status. To prove status, U.S. citizens or nationals must attach a copy of a document proving status, such as a U.S. passport, birth certificate, or certificate of naturalization, and lawful permanent residents must attach a copy of both sides of their Alien Registration Card (Form I-551).

The determination of your eligibility to sponsor an immigrant will be based on an evaluation of your demonstrated ability to maintain an annual income at or above 125 percent of the Federal poverty line (100 percent if you are a petitioner sponsoring your spouse or child and you are on active duty in the U.S. Armed Forces). The assessment of your ability to maintain an adequate income will include your current employment, household size, and household income as shown on the Federal income tax returns for the 3 most recent tax years. Assets that are readily converted to cash and that can be made available for the support of sponsored immigrants if necessary, including any such assets of the immigrant(s) you are sponsoring, may also be considered.

The greatest weight in determining eligibility will be placed on current employment and household income. If a petitioner is unable to demonstrate ability to meet the stated income and asset requirements, a joint sponsor who *can* meet the income and asset requirements is needed. Failure to provide adequate evidence of income and/or assets or an affidavit of support completed by a joint sponsor will result in denial of the immigrant's application for an immigrant visa or adjustment to permanent resident status.

A. Sponsor's Employment

I am:
1. Employed by _____ *(Provide evidence of employment)*
   Annual salary $ _____ *or* hourly wage $ _____ *(for _____ hours per week)*
2. Self employed _____ *(Name of business)*
   Nature of employment or business _____
3. Unemployed or retired since _____

B. Use of Benefits

Have you or anyone related to you by birth, marriage, or adoption living in your household or listed as a dependent on your most recent income tax return received any type of means-tested public benefit in the past 3 years?
   Yes ____ No ____ *(If yes, provide details, including program and dates, on a separate sheet of paper)*

C. Sponsor's Household Size

	Number
1. Number of persons (related to you by birth, marriage, or adoption) living in your residence, including yourself. *(Do NOT include persons being sponsored in this affidavit.)*	_____
2. Number of immigrants being sponsored in this affidavit *(Include all persons in Part 3.)*	_____
3. Number of immigrants **NOT** living in your household whom you are still obligated to support under a previously signed affidavit of support using Form I-864.	_____
4. Number of persons who are otherwise dependent on you, as claimed in your tax return for the most recent tax year.	_____
5. Total household size. *(Add lines 1 through 4.)* **Total**	_____

List persons below who are included in lines 1 or 3 for whom you previously have submitted INS Form I-864, *if your support obligation has not terminated.*

(If additional space is needed, use additional paper)

Name	A-Number	Date Affidavit of Support Signed	Relationship

123

Form I-864 (10/6/97) Page 2

D. Sponsor's Annual Household Income

Enter total unadjusted income from your Federal income tax return for the most recent tax year below.   If you last filed a joint income tax return but are using only your *own* income to qualify, list total earnings from your W-2 Forms, or, *if* necessary to reach the required income for your household size, include income from other sources listed on your tax return.   If your *individual* income does not meet the income requirement for your household size, you may also list total income for anyone related to you by birth, marriage, or adoption currently living with you in your residence if they have lived in your residence for the previous 6 months, or any person shown as a dependent on your Federal income tax return for the most recent tax year, even if not living in the household.   For their income to be considered, household members or dependents must be willing to make their income available for support of the sponsored immigrant(s) and to complete and sign Form I-864A, Contract Between Sponsor and Household Member.   A sponsored immigrant/household member only need   complete Form I-864A if his or her income will be used to determine your ability to support a spouse and/or children immigrating with him or her.

You must attach evidence of current employment and copies of income tax returns as filed with the IRS for the most recent 3 tax years for yourself and all persons whose income is listed below.   See "Required Evidence" in Instructions. Income from all 3 years will be considered in determining your ability to support the immigrant(s) you are sponsoring.

I filed a single/separate tax return for the most recent tax year.

I filed a joint return for the most recent tax year which includes only my own income.

I filed a joint return for the most recent tax year which includes income for my spouse and myself.

   I am submitting documentation of my individual income (Forms W-2 and 1099).

   I am qualifying using my spouse's income; my spouse is submitting a Form I-864A.

Indicate most recent tax year _____ *(tax year)*

Sponsor's individual income $ _____

or

Sponsor and spouse's combined income $ _____
(If joint tax return filed; spouse must submit Form I-864A.)

Income of other qualifying persons.
(List names; include spouse if applicable. Each person must complete Form I-864A.)

_____ $ _____

_____ $ _____

_____ $ _____

Total Household Income $ _____

Explain on separate sheet of paper if you or any of the above listed individuals are submitting Federal income tax returns for fewer than 3 years, or if other explanation of income, employment, or evidence is necessary.

E. Determination of Eligibility Based on Income

1.   I am subject to the 125 percent of poverty line requirement for sponsors.
    I am subject to the 100 percent of poverty line requirement for sponsors on active duty in the U.S. Armed Forces sponsoring their spouse or child.

2.   Sponsor's total household size, from Part 4.C., line 5 _____.

3.   Minimum income requirement from the Poverty Guidelines chart for the year of _____ is $ _____
    for this household size.   *(year)*

If you are currently employed and your household income for your household size is equal to or greater than the applicable poverty line requirement (from line E.3.), you do not need to list assets (Parts 4.F. and 5) or have a joint sponsor (Part 6) unless you are requested to do so by a Consular or Immigration Officer.   You may skip to Part 7, Use of the Affidavit of Support to Overcome Public Charge Ground of Admissibility.   Otherwise, you should continue with Part 4.F.

F. Sponsor's Assets and Liabilities

Your assets and those of your qualifying household members and dependents may be used to demonstrate ability to maintain an income at or above 125 percent (or 100 percent, if applicable) of the poverty line *if* they are available for the support of the sponsored immigrant(s) and can readily be converted into cash within 1 year. The household member, other than the immigrant(s) you are sponsoring, must complete and sign Form I-864A, Contract Between Sponsor and Household Member. List the cash value of each asset *after* any debts or liens are subtracted. Supporting evidence must be attached to establish location, ownership, date of acquisition, and value of each asset listed, including any liens and liabilities related to each asset listed. See "Evidence of Assets" in Instructions.

Type of Asset	Cash Value of Assets (Subtract any debts)
Savings deposits	$
Stocks, bonds, certificates of deposit	$
Life insurance cash value	$
Real estate	$
Other (specify)	$
Total Cash Value of Assets	$_____

Part 5. Immigrant's Assets and Offsetting Liabilities

The sponsored immigrant's assets may also be used in support of your ability to maintain income at or above 125 percent of the poverty line *if* the assets are or will be available in the United States for the support of the sponsored immigrant(s) and can readily be converted into cash within 1 year.

The sponsored immigrant should provide information on his or her assets in a format similar to part 4.F. above. Supporting evidence must be attached to establish location, ownership, and value of each asset listed, including any liens and liabilities for each asset listed. See "Evidence of Assets" in Instructions.

Part 6. Joint Sponsors

If household income and assets do not meet the appropriate poverty line for your household size, a joint sponsor is required. There may be more than one joint sponsor, but each joint sponsor must individually meet the 125 percent of poverty line requirement based on his or her household income and/or assets, including any assets of the sponsored immigrant. By submitting a separate Affidavit of Support under Section 213A of the Act (Form I-864), a joint sponsor accepts joint responsibility with the petitioner for the sponsored immigrant(s) until they become U.S. citizens, can be credited with 40 quarters of work, leave the United States permanently, or die.

Part 7. Use of the Affidavit of Support to Overcome Public Charge Ground of Inadmissibility

Section 212(a)(4)(C) of the Immigration and Nationality Act provides that an alien seeking permanent residence as an immediate relative (including an orphan), as a family-sponsored immigrant, or as an alien who will accompany or follow to join another alien is considered to be likely to become a public charge and is inadmissible to the United States unless a sponsor submits a legally enforceable affidavit of support on behalf of the alien. Section 212(a)(4)(D) imposes the same requirement on an employment-based immigrant, and those aliens who accompany or follow to join the employment-based immigrant, if the employment-based immigrant will be employed by a relative, or by a firm in which a relative owns a significant interest. Separate affidavits of support are required for family members at the time they immigrate if they are not included on this affidavit of support or do not apply for an immigrant visa or adjustment of status within 6 months of the date this affidavit of support is originally signed. The sponsor must provide the sponsored immigrant(s) whatever support is necessary to maintain them at an income that is at least 125 percent of the Federal poverty guidelines.

I submit this affidavit of support in consideration of the sponsored immigrant(s) not being found inadmissible to the United States under section 212(a)(4)(C) (or 212(a)(4)(D) for an employment-based immigrant) and to enable the sponsored immigrant(s) to overcome this ground of inadmissibility. I agree to provide the sponsored immigrant(s) whatever support is necessary to maintain the sponsored immigrant(s) at an income that is at least 125 percent of the Federal poverty guidelines. I understand that my obligation will continue until my death or the sponsored immigrant(s) have become U.S. citizens, can be credited with 40 quarters of work, depart the United States permanently, or die.

Notice of Change of Address.

Sponsors are required to provide written notice of any change of address within 30 days of the change in address until the sponsored immigrant(s) have become U.S. citizens, can be credited with 40 quarters of work, depart the United States permanently, or die. To comply with this requirement, the sponsor must complete INS Form I-865. Failure to give this notice may subject the sponsor to the civil penalty established under section 213A(d)(2) which ranges from $250 to $2,000, unless the failure to report occurred with the knowledge that the sponsored immigrant(s) had received means-tested public benefits, in which case the penalty ranges from $2,000 to $5,000.

If my address changes for any reason before my obligations under this affidavit of support terminate, I will complete and file INS Form I-865, Sponsor's Notice of Change of Address, within 30 days of the change of address. I understand that failure to give this notice may subject me to civil penalties.

Means-tested Public Benefit Prohibitions and Exceptions.

Under section 403(a) of Public Law 104-193 (Welfare Reform Act), aliens lawfully admitted for permanent residence in the United States, with certain exceptions, are ineligible for most Federally-funded means-tested public benefits during their first 5 years in the United States. This provision does not apply to public benefits specified in section 403(c) of the Welfare Reform Act or to State public benefits, including emergency Medicaid; short-term, non-cash emergency relief; services provided under the National School Lunch and Child Nutrition Acts; immunizations and testing and treatment for communicable diseases; student assistance under the Higher Education Act and the Public Health Service Act; certain forms of foster-care or adoption assistance under the Social Security Act; Head Start programs; means-tested programs under the Elementary and Secondary Education Act; and Job Training Partnership Act programs.

Consideration of Sponsor's Income in Determining Eligibility for Benefits.

If a permanent resident alien is no longer statutorily barred from a federally-funded means-tested public benefit program and applies for such a benefit, the income and resources of the sponsor and the sponsor's spouse will be considered (or deemed) to be the income and resources of the sponsored immigrant in determining the immigrant's eligibility for Federal means-tested public benefits. Any State or local government may also choose to consider (or deem) the income and resources of the sponsor and the sponsor's spouse to be the income and resources of the immigrant for the purposes of determining eligibility for their means-tested public benefits. The attribution of the income and resources of the sponsor and the sponsor's spouse to the immigrant will continue until the immigrant becomes a U.S. citizen or has worked or can be credited with 40 qualifying quarters of work, provided that the immigrant or the worker crediting the quarters to the immigrant has not received any Federal means-tested public benefit during any creditable quarter for any period after December 31, 1996.

I understand that, under section 213A of the Immigration and Nationality Act (the Act), as amended, this affidavit of support constitutes a contract between me and the U.S. Government. This contract is designed to protect the United States Government, and State and local government agencies or private entities that provide means-tested public benefits, from having to pay benefits to or on behalf of the sponsored immigrant(s), for as long as I am obligated to support them under this affidavit of support. I understand that the sponsored immigrants, or any Federal, State, local, or private entity that pays any means-tested benefit to or on behalf of the sponsored immigrant(s), are entitled to sue me if I fail to meet my obligations under this affidavit of support, as defined by section 213A and INS regulations.

Civil Action to Enforce.

If the immigrant on whose behalf this affidavit of support is executed receives any Federal, State, or local means-tested public benefit before this obligation terminates, the Federal, State, or local agency or private entity may request reimbursement from the sponsor who signed this affidavit. If the sponsor fails to honor the request for reimbursement, the agency may sue the sponsor in any U.S. District Court or any State court with jurisdiction of civil actions for breach of contract. INS will provide names, addresses, and Social Security account numbers of sponsors to benefit-providing agencies for this purpose. Sponsors may also be liable for paying the costs of collection, including legal fees.

I acknowledge that section 213A(a)(1)(B) of the Act grants the sponsored immigrant(s) and any Federal, State, local, or private agency that pays any means-tested public benefit to or on behalf of the sponsored immigrant(s) standing to sue me for failing to meet my obligations under this affidavit of support. I agree to submit to the personal jurisdiction of any court of the United States or of any State, territory, or possession of the United States if the court has subject matter jurisdiction of a civil lawsuit to enforce this affidavit of support. I agree that no lawsuit to enforce this affidavit of support shall be barred by any statute of limitations that might otherwise apply, so long as the plaintiff initiates the civil lawsuit no later than ten (10) years after the date on which a sponsored immigrant last received any means-tested public benefits.

Collection of Judgment.

I acknowledge that a plaintiff may seek specific performance of my support obligation. Furthermore, any money judgment against me based on this affidavit of support may be collected through the use of a judgment lien under 28 U.S.C. 3201, a writ of execution under 28 U.S.C. 3203, a judicial installment payment order under 28 U.S.C. 3204, garnishment under 28 U.S.C. 3205, or through the use of any corresponding remedy under State law. I may also be held liable for costs of collection, including attorney fees.

Concluding Provisions.

I, _____, certify under penalty of perjury under the laws of the United States that:

  (a) *I know the contents of this affidavit of support signed by me;*
  (b) *All the statements in this affidavit of support are true and correct;*
  (c) *I make this affidavit of support for the consideration stated in Part 7, freely and without any mental reservation or purpose of evasion;*
  (d) *Income tax returns submitted in support of this affidavit are true copies of the returns filed with the Internal Revenue Service; and*
  (e) *Any other evidence submitted is true and correct.*

_____   _____
            (Sponsor's Signature)   (Date)

Subscribed and sworn to *(or affirmed)* before me this

_____day of _____, _____
                          (Month)   (Year)

at _____.

My commission expires on _____.

_____
(Signature of Notary Public or Officer Administering Oath)

_____
                             (Title)

Part 8.   If someone other than the sponsor prepared this affidavit of support, that person must complete the following:

I certify under penalty of perjury under the laws of the United States that I prepared this affidavit of support at the sponsor's request, and that this affidavit of support is based on all information of which I have knowledge.

Signature	Print Your Name	Date	Daytime Telephone Number
			( )

Firm Name and Address

START HERE - Please Type or Print

Part 1. Information about the person or organization filing this petition.

If an individual is filing, use the top Name line. Organization should use the second line.

Family Name	Given Name	Middle Initial

Company or Organization

Address - Attn:

Street Number and Name		Room #
City	State or Province	
Country	ZIP/Postal Code	

IRS Tax #	Social Security #

Part 2. Petition Type.   This petition is being filed for: (check one)

- a. ☐ An alien of extraordinary ability
- b. ☐ An outstanding professor or researcher
- c. ☐ A multinational executive or manager
- d. ☐ A member of the professions holding an advanced degree or an alien of exceptional ability
- e. ☐ A skilled worker (requiring at least two years of specialized training or experience) or professional
- f. ☐ An employee of a U.S business operating in Hong Kong
- g. ☐ Any other worker (requiring less than two years training or experience)

Part 3. Information about the person you are filing for.

Family Name	Given Name	Middle Initial

Address - C/O

Street # and Name		Apt. #
City	State or Province	
Country	ZIP or Postal Code	

Date of Birth (month/day/year)	Country of Birth
Social Security # (if any)	A# (if any)

If in the U.S.	Date of Arrival (month/day/year)	I-94
	Current Nonimmigrant Status	Expires on (month/day/year)

Part 4. Processing Information.

Below give the U.S. Consulate you want notified if this petition is approved and if any requested adjustment of status cannot be granted.

U.S Consulate: City   Country

Form I-140 (Rev. 12-2-91)   *Continued on back.*

128

FOR INS USE ONLY

Returned	Receipt

Resubmitted

Reloc Sent

Reloc Rec'd

☐ Petitioner Interviewed
☐ Beneficiary Interviewed

Classification
- ☐ 203(b)(1)(A) Alien Of Extraordinary Ability
- ☐ 203(b)(1)(B) Outstanding Professor or Researcher
- ☐ 203(b)(1)(C) Multi-national executive or manager
- ☐ 203(b)(2) Member of profession w/adv. degree or of exceptional ability
- ☐ 203(b)(3)(A)(i) Skilled worker
- ☐ 203(b)(3)(A)(ii) Professional
- ☐ 203(b)(3)(A)(iii) Other worker
- ☐ Sec. 124 IMMACT-Employee of U.S. business in Hong Kong

Priority Date	Consulate

Remarks

Action Block

To Be Completed by Attorney or Representative, if any

☐ Fill in box if G-28 is attached to represent the petitioner

VOLAG#

ATTY State License #

Part 4. Processing Information. *(continued)*

you gave a U. S. address in Part 3, print the person's foreign address below. If his/her native alphabet does not use Roman letters, print his/her name and
ign address in the native alphabet.

ne   Address

you filing any other petitions or applications with this one?		☐ No	☐ yes attach an explanation
e person you are filing for in exclusion or deportation proceedings?		☐ No	☐ yes attach an explanation
an immigrant visa petition ever been filed by or in behalf of this person?		☐ No	☐ yes attach an explanation

Part 5. Additional Information about the employer.

e of petitioner
(eck one)

☐ Self   ☐ Individual U.S. Citizen   ☐ Company or organization

☐ Permanent Resident   ☐ Other explain_____

company, give the following:
   Type of business

Date Established	Current # of employees	Gross Annual Income	Net Annual Income

n individual, give the following: Annual Income
   Occupation

Part 6. Basic information about the proposed employment.

	Nontechnical description of job

ress where the person will work
fferent from address in Part 1.

is a full-time
tion?   ☐ yes   ☐ No (hours per week _____   Wages per week

is a permanent position?   ☐ yes ☐ No   Is this a new position? ☐ yes ☐ No

Part 7. Information on spouse and all children of the person you are filing for.

ide an attachment listing the family members of the person you are filing for. Be sure to include their full name, relationship, date and country of birth, and
ent address.

Part 8. Signature. *Read the information on penalties in the instructions before completing this section.*

tify under penalty of perjury under the laws of the United States of America that this petition, and the evidence submitted with it, is all true and correct. I
orize the release of any information from my records which the Immigration and Naturalization Service needs to determine eligibility for the benefit I am
ing.

nature   Date

se Note: *If you do not completely fill out this form, or fail to submit required documents listed in the instructions, you cannot be found eligible
he requested document and this application may be denied.*

Part 9. Signature of person preparing form if other than above. *(Sign below)*

lare that I prepared this application at the request of the above person and it is based on all information of which I have knowledge.

nature   Print Your Name   Date

Name
Address

* U.S. GPO:1992-312-328/51143

I-140 (Rev. 12-2-91)

U.S. Department of Justice
Immigration and Naturalization Service

Application to Register Permanent Residence or Adjust Statu

OMB No. 1115-005

START HERE - Please Type or Print

Part 1. Information about you.

Family Name	Given Name	Middle Initial

Address - C/O

Street Number and Name	Apt. #

City

State	Zip Code

Date of Birth (month/day/year)	Country of Birth

Social Security #	A # (if any)

Date of Last Arrival (month/day/year)	I-94#

Current INS Status	Expires on (month/day/year)

Part 2. Application Type. *(check one)*

I am applying for adjustment to permanent resident status because:

a. ☐ an immigrant petition giving me an immediately available immigrant visa number has been approved (attach a copy of the approval notice, or a relative, special immigrant juvenile, or special immigrant military visa petition filed with this application will give me an immediately available visa number if approved.

b. ☐ My spouse or parent applied for adjustment of status or was granted lawful permanent residence in an immigrant visa category which allows derivative status for spouses and children.

c. ☐ I entered as a K-1 fiance(e) of a U.S. citizen whom I married within 90 days of entry, or I am the K-2 child of such a fiance(e) (attach a copy of the fiance(e) petition approval notice and the marriage certificate).

d. ☐ I was granted asylum or derivative asylum status as the spouse or child of a person granted asylum and am eligible for adjustment.

e. ☐ I am a native or citizen of Cuba admitted or paroled into the U.S. after January 1, 1959, and thereafter have been physically present in the U.S. for at least 1 year.

f. ☐ I am the husband, wife, or minor unmarried child of a Cuban described in (e) and am residing with that person, and was admitted or paroled into the U.S. after January 1, 1959, and thereafter have been physically present in the U.S. for at least 1 year.

g. ☐ I have continuously resided in the U.S. since before January 1, 1972.

h. ☐ Other-explain_____

I am already a permanent resident and am applying to have the date I was granted permanent residence adjusted to the date I originally arrived in the U.S. as a nonimmigrant or parolee, or as of May 2, 1964, whichever is later, and: *(Check one)*

i. ☐ I am a native citizen of Cuba and meet the description in (e), above.

j. ☐ I am the husband, wife or minor unmarried child of a Cuban, and meet the description in (f), above.

FOR INS USE ONLY

Returned	Receipt

Resubmitted

Reloc Sent

Reloc Rec'd

☐ Applicant Interviewed

Section of Law
- ☐ Sec. 209(b), INA
- ☐ Sec. 13, Act of 9/11/57
- ☐ Sec. 245, INA
- ☐ Sec. 249, INA
- ☐ Sec. 1 Act of 11/2/66
- ☐ Sec. 2 Act of 11/2/66
- ☐ Other_____

Country Chargeable

Eligibility Under Sec. 245
- ☐ Approved Visa Petition
- ☐ Dependent of Principal Alien
- ☐ Special Immigrant
- ☐ Other_____

Preference

Action Block

To Be Completed by Attorney or Representative, if any

☐ Fill in box if G-28 is attached to represent the applicant

VOLAG#

ATTY State License #

Form I-485 (09-09-92)N   *Continued on back*

Part 3. Processing Information.

City/Town/Village of birth	Current occupation
ur mother's first name	Your father's first name

ve your name exactly how it appears on your Arrival /Departure Record (Form I-94)

ce of last entry into the U.S. (City/State)	In what status did you last enter? *(Visitor, Student, exchange alien, crewman, temporary worker, without inspection, etc.)*
ere you inspected by a U.S. Immigration Officer? ☐ Yes ☐ No	
onimmigrant Visa Number	Consulate where Visa was issued
te Visa was issued (onth/day/year) Sex: ☐ Male ☐ Female	Marital Status: ☐ Married ☐ Single ☐ Divorced ☐ Widowed

ve you ever before applied for permanent resident status in the U.S.? ☐ No ☐ Yes (give date and place of filing and final disposition):

List your present husband/wife, all of your sons and daughters (if you have none, write "none". If additional space is needed, use separate paper).

nily ne	Given Name	Middle Initial	Date of Birth (month/day/year)
untry of birth	Relationship	A #	Applying with you? ☐ Yes ☐ No
nily ne	Given Name	Middle Initial	Date of Birth (month/day/year)
untry of birth	Relationship	A #	Applying with you? ☐ Yes ☐ No
nily ne	Given Name	Middle Initial	Date of Birth (month/day/year)
untry of birth	Relationship	A #	Applying with you? ☐ Yes ☐ No
nily ne	Given Name	Middle Initial	Date of Birth (month/day/year)
untry of birth	Relationship	A #	Applying with you? ☐ Yes ☐ No
nily ne	Given Name	Middle Initial	Date of Birth (month/day/year)
untry of birth	Relationship	A #	Applying with you? ☐ Yes ☐ No

List your present and past membership in or affiliation with every political organization, association, fund, foundation, party, club, society, or similar group in the United States or in any other place since your 16th birthday. Include any foreign military service in this part. If none, write "none". Include the name of organization, location, dates of membership from and to, and the nature of the organization. If additional space is needed, use separate paper.

_____

_____

_____

_____

_____

_____

orm I-485 (Rev. 09-09-92) N

Part 3. Processing Information. *(Continued)*

Please answer the following questions. (If your answer is "**Yes**" on any one of these questions, explain on a separate piece of paper. Answering "**Yes**" does not necessarily mean that you are not entitled to register for permanent residence or adjust status).

1. Have you ever, in or outside the U. S.:
   a. knowingly committed any crime of moral turpitude or a drug-related offense for which you have not been arrested?
   b. been arrested, cited, charged, indicted, fined, or imprisoned for breaking or violating any law or ordinance, excluding traffic violations?
   c. been the beneficiary of a pardon, amnesty, rehabilitation decree, other act of clemency or similar action?
   d. exercised diplomatic immunity to avoid prosecution for a criminal offense in the U.S.?　☐ Yes ☐ No

2. Have you received public assistance in the U.S. from any source, including the U.S. government or any state, county, city, or municipality (other than emergency medical treatment) , or are you likely to receive public assistance in the future?　☐ Yes ☐ No

3. Have you ever:
   a. within the past 10 years been a prostitute or procured anyone for prostitution, or intend to engage in such activities in the future?
   b. engaged in any unlawful commercialized vice, including, but not limited to, illegal gambling?
   c. knowingly encouraged, induced, assisted, abetted or aided any alien to try to enter the U.S. illegally?
   d. illicitly trafficked in any controlled substance, or knowingly assisted, abetted or colluded in the illicit trafficking of any controlled substance?　☐ Yes ☐ No

4. Have you ever engaged in, conspired to engage in, or do you intend to engage in, or have you ever solicited membership or funds for, or have you through any means ever assisted or provided any type of material support to, any person or organization that has ever engaged or conspired to engage, in sabotage, kidnapping, political assassination, hijacking, or any other form of terrorist activity?　☐ Yes ☐ No

5. Do you intend to engage in the U.S. in:
   a. espionage?
   b. any activity a purpose of which is opposition to, or the control or overthrow of, the Government of the United States, by force, violence or other unlawful means?
   c. any activity to violate or evade any law prohibiting the export from the United States of goods, technology or sensitive information?　☐ Yes ☐ No

6. Have you ever been a member of, or in any way affiliated with, the Communist Party or any other totalitarian party?　☐ Yes ☐ No

7. Did you, during the period March 23, 1933 to May 8, 1945, in association with either the Nazi Government of Germany or any organization or government associated or allied with the Nazi Government of Germany, ever order, incite, assist or otherwise participate in the persecution of any person because of race, religion, national origin or political opinion?　☐ Yes ☐ No

8. Have you ever engaged in genocide, or otherwise ordered, incited, assisted or otherwise participated in the killing of any person because of race, religion, nationality, ethnic origin, or political opinion?　☐ Yes ☐ No

9. Have you ever been deported from the U.S., or removed from the U.S. at government expense, excluded within the past year, or are you now in exclusion or deportation proceedings?　☐ Yes ☐ No

10. Are you under a final order of civil penalty for violating section 274C of the Immigration Act for use of fraudulent documents, or have you, by fraud or willful misrepresentation of a material fact, ever sought to procure, or procured, a visa, other documentation, entry into the U.S., or any other immigration benefit?　☐ Yes ☐ No

11. Have you ever left the U.S. to avoid being drafted into the U.S. Armed Forces?　☐ Yes ☐ No

12. Have you ever been a J nonimmigrant exchange visitor who was subject to the 2 year foreign residence requirement and not yet complied with that requirement or obtained a waiver?　☐ Yes ☐ No

13. Are you now withholding custody of a U.S. Citizen child outside the U.S. from a person granted custody of the child?　☐ Yes ☐ No

14. Do you plan to practice polygamy in the U.S.?　☐ Yes ☐ No

rt 4. Signature. *(Read the information on penalties in the instructions before completing this section. You must file this application while in the United States.)*

tify under penalty of perjury under the laws of the United States of America that this application, and the evidence submitted with it, is all true and correct. I orize the release of any information from my records which the Immigration and Naturalization Service needs to determine eligibility for the benefit I am king.

nature	**Print Your Name**	**Date**	**Daytime Phone Number**

ase Note:*If you do not completely fill out this form, or fail to submit required documents listed in the instructions, you may not be found eligible for the requested document and this application may be denied.*

rt 5. Signature of person preparing form if other than above. *(Sign Below)*

clare that I prepared this application at the request of the above person and it is based on all information of which I have knowledge.

nature	**Print Your Name**	**Date**	**Day time Phone Number**

n Name
Address

SAMPLE

133

m I-485 (Rev. 09-09-92) N

START HERE - Please Type or Print

Part 1. Information about Applicant

Family Name	First Name	Middle Name

Address - C/O

Street Number and Name		Apt. Suite
City	State or Province	
Country		ZIP/Postal Code
INS A#	Date of Birth (month/day/year)	Country of Birth

Part 2. Basis for Eligibility (check one)

1. On Form I-485, Part 2, I checked application type (check one):

a. ☐ An immigrant petition . . . **Go to #2.**
b. ☐ My spouse or parent applied . . . **Go to #2.**
c. ☐ I entered as a K-1 fiance . . . **Stop Here. Do Not File This Form.**
d. ☐ I was granted asylum . . . **Stop Here. Do Not File This Form.**
e. ☐ I am a native or citizen of Cuba . . **Stop Here. Do Not File This Form.**
f. ☐ I am the spouse or child of a Cuban **Stop Here. Do Not File This Form.**
g. ☐ I have continuously resided in the U.S. . **Stop Here. Do Not File This Form.**
h. ☐ Other . . . **Go to #2.**
i. ☐ I am already a permanent resident . . . **Stop Here. Do Not File This Form.**
j. ☐ I am already a permanent resident and am the spouse or child of a Cuban **Stop Here. Do Not File This Form.**

2. I have filed Form I-360; and I am applying for adjustment of status as a special immigrant juvenile court dependent (check one):

☐ Yes **Stop Here. Do Not File This Form.**   ☐ No **Go to #3.**

3. I have filed Form I-360; and I am applying for adjustment of status as a special immigrant who has served in the United States Armed Forces (check one):

☐ Yes **Stop Here. Do Not File This Form.**   ☐ No **Go to #4.**

4. I last entered the United States (check one):

☐ Legally as a crewman (D-1/D-2 visa). **Go to #11.**   ☐ Legally without a visa **Go to #5.**
☐ Without inspection. **Go to #11.**   ☐ Legally as a parolee. **Go to #5.**
☐ Legally in transit without visa status. **Go to #11.**   ☐ Legally with another type of visa (show type _____) **Go to #5.**

5. I last entered the United States legally without a visa as a visitor for tourism or business; and I am applying for adjustment of status as the spouse, unmarried child less than 21 years old, parent, widow or widower of a United States citizen (check one):

☐ Yes **Stop Here. Do Not File This Form.**   ☐ No **Go to #6.**

6. I last entered the United States legally as a parolee, or with a visa (except as a crewman), or as a Canadian citizen without a visa; and I am applying for adjustment of status (check one):

☐ As the spouse, unmarried child less than 21 years old, parent, widow or widower of a United States citizen, **Stop Here. Do Not File This Form.**

☐ As a special immigrant retired international organization employee or family member of an international organization employee or as a special immigrant physician; and I have filed Form I-360. **Stop Here. Do Not File This Form.**

☐ Under some other category. **Go to #7.**

7. I am a national of the (former) Soviet Union, Vietnam, Laos or Cambodia who last entered the United States legally as a public interest parolee after having been denied refugee status; and I am applying for adjustment of status under Public Law 101-167 (*check one*):

   ☐ Yes **Stop Here. Do Not File This Form.** ☐ No **Go to #8.**

8. I have been employed in the United States after 01/01/77 without INS authorization (*check one*):

   ☐ Yes **Go to #9.** ☐ No **Go to #10.**

9. I am applying for adjustment of status under the Immigration Nursing Relief Act (INRA); I was employed without INS authorization only on or before 11/29/90; and I have always maintained a lawful immigration status while in the United States after 11/05/86 (*check one*):

   ☐ Yes **Stop Here. Do Not File This Form.** ☐ No **Go to #10.**

10. I am now in lawful immigration status; and I have always maintained a lawful immigration status while in the United States after 11/05/86 (*check one*):

    ☐ Yes **Stop Here. Do Not File This Form .**
    ☐ No, but I believe that INS will determine that my failure to be in or maintain a lawful immigration status was through no fault of my own or for technical reasons. **Stop Here. Do Not File This Form,** and attach an explanation to your Form I-485 application.
    ☐ No **Go to #11.**

11. I am unmarried and less than 17 years old (*check one*):

    ☐ Yes **Stop Here. File This Form and Form I-485.** Pay only the fee required with Form I-485.
    ☐ No **Go to #12.**

12. I am the unmarried child of a legalized alien and am less than 21 years old, or I am the spouse of a legalized alien; and I have attached a copy of my receipt or approval notice showing that I have properly filed Form I-817 Application for Voluntary Departure under the Family Unity Program (*check one*):

    ☐ Yes **Stop Here. File This Form and Form I-485.** Pay only the fee required with Form I-485.
    ☐ No **Go to #13.**

13. **File This Form and Form I-485. You must pay the additional sum:**

    $130.00 - Fee required with Form I-485* and
    $650.00 - Additional sum under section 245(i) of the Act
    ─────
    $780.00 - Total amount you must pay.

*If you filed Form I-485 separately, attach a copy of your filing receipt and pay only the additional sum of $650.00. In #11 and /or #12, show the answer you would have given on the date you filed Form I-485.

Part 3. Signature. Read the information on penalties in the instructions before completing this section. If someone helped you prepare this petition he or she must complete Part 4.

I certify, under penalty of perjury under the laws of the United States of America, that this application, and the evidence submitted with it, is all true and correct. I authorize the release of any information from my records which the Immigration and Naturalization Service needs to determine eligibility for the benefit I am seeking.

Signature	Print Your Name	Date	Daytime Telephone No.

Please Note: If you do not completely fill out this form or fail to submit required documents listed in the instructions, you may not be found eligible for the requested document and this application may be denied.

Part 4. Signature of person preparing form if other than above. (*Sign Below*)

I declare that I prepared this application at the request of the above person and it is based on all information of which I have knowledge.

Signature	Print Your Name	Date	Daytime Telephone No.

Firm Name
and Address

Form I-485 (09/30/94) Supplement A

START HERE - Please Type or Print

Part 1.   Information about you.

Family Name	Given Name	Middle Initial

Address - In Care of:

Street # and Name		Apt. #

City or town	State or Province

Country	Zip or Postal Code

Date of Birth (month/day/year)	Country of Birth

Social Security #	A#

If in the U.S.	Date of Arrival (month/day/year)	I-94#
	Current Nonimmigrant Status	Expires on (month/day/year)

Part 2.   Application Type (check one).

a. ☐ This petition is based on an investment in a commercial enterprise in a targeted employment area for which the required amount of capital invested has been adjusted downward.

b. ☐ This petition is based on an investment in a commercial enterprise in an area for which the required amount of capital invested has been adjusted upward.

b. ☐ This petition is based on an investment in a commercial enterprise which is not in either a targeted area or in an upward adjustment area.

Part 3.   Information about your investment.

Name of Commercial Enterprise Invested In

Street Address

Phone #	Business Organized as (Corporation, partnership, etc...)

Kind of Business
(Example: Furniture Manufacturer)

Date established (month/day/year)	IRS Tax #

Date of your initial Investment(month/day/year)	Amount of your Initial Investment $

Your total Capital Investment in Enterprise to date $	% of Enterprise you own

If you are not the sole investor in the new commercial enterprise, list on separate paper the names of all other parties (natural and non-natural) who hold a percentage share of ownership of the new enterprise and indicate whether any of these parties is seeking classifications as an alien entrepreneur. Include the name, percentage of ownership and whether or not the person is seeking classification under section 203(b)(5).

If you indicated in Part 2 that the enterprise was in a targeted employment area or in an upward adjustment area, give the location at right.   County   State

FOR INS USE ONLY

Returned	Receipt
Resubmitted	
Reloc Sent	
Reloc Rec'd	
☐ Applicant Interviewed	

Action Block

To Be Completed by
Attorney or Representative, if any
☐ Fill in box if G-28 is attached to represent the applicant

VOLAG#

ATTY State License #

Form I-526 (Rev. 12-2-91)

Part 4. Additional information about the enterprise.

Type of enterprise (check one):
- ☐ new commercial enterprise resulting from the creation of a new business
- ☐ new commercial enterprise resulting from the reorganization of an existing business.
- ☐ new commercial enterprise resulting from a capital investment in an existing business.

Assets:

Total amount in U.S. bank account		$ _____
Total value of all assets purchased for use in the enterprise		$ _____
Total value of all property transferred from abroad to the new enterprise		$ _____
Total of all debt financing		$ _____
Total stock purchases		$ _____
Other (explain on separate paper)		$ _____
Total		$ _____

Income:

When you made investment	Gross	$ _____	Net	$ _____
Now	Gross	$ _____	Net	$ _____

Net worth:

When you made investment	$ _____	Now	$ _____

Part 5. Employment creation information.

Number of full-time employees in Enterprise in U.S. (excluding you, spouse, sons & daughters)

When you made you initial investment _____ Now _____ Difference _____

How many of these new jobs were created by your investment? _____ How many additional new jobs will be created by your additional investment? _____

What is your position, office or title with the new commercial enterprise?

_____

Briefly describe your duties, activities and responsibilities.

_____

_____

_____

Your Salary _____ Cost of Benefits _____

Part 6. Processing information.

Below give the U.S. Consulate you want notified if this petition is approved and if any requested adjustment of status cannot be granted.

American Consulate: City _____ Country _____

If you gave a U.S. address in Part 1, print your foreign address below. If your native alphabet does not use Roman letters, print your name and foreign address in the native alphabet.

Name _____ Foreign Address _____

Is application for adjustment of status attached to this petition?	☐ yes		☐ no
Are you in exclusion or deportation proceeding?	☐ yes (If yes, explain on separate paper)		☐ no
Have you ever worked in the U.S. without permission?	☐ yes (explain on separate paper)		☐ no

Part 7. Signature. *Read the information on penalties in the instructions before completing this section.*

I certify under penalty of perjury under the laws of the United States of America that this petition, and the evidence submitted with it, is all true and correct. I authorize the release of any information from my records which the Immigration and Naturalization Service needs to determine eligibility for the benefit I am seeking.

Signature _____ Date _____

Please Note: If you do not completely fill out this form, or fail to submit required documents listed in the instruction, you may not be found eligible for the requested document and this application may be denied.

Part 8. Signature of person preparing form if other than above. *(Sign below)*

I declare that I prepared this application at the request of the above person and it is based on all information of which I have knowledge.

Signature _____ Print Your Name _____ Date _____

Name _____
Address _____

Form I-526 (Rev. 12-2-91)

U.S. Department of Justice
Immigration and Naturalization Service

Application by Nonimmigrant Student for Extension of Stay, School Transfer, or Permission to Accept or Continue Employment

OMB #1115 0060

I am an:	For Official Use Only	Date of Action
☐ F-1 Student ☐ M-1 Student	☐ Extension Granted ☐ Extension Denied	DD or OIC Office
I am applying for: ☐ Extension of stay ☐ School transfer ☐ Off-campus employment due to economic necessity ☐ Practical training	☐ Transfer Granted ☐ Transfer Denied ☐ Employment Granted ☐ Employment Denied ☐ Practical Training Granted ☐ Practical Training Denied	
☐ Prior to completion of studies ☐ Curricular or work/study ☐ Post completion of studies	From To (or VD to)	

A. This Section to be completed by all applicants.

1. Name (Family in CAPS)   (First)   (Middle)

2. U.S. Address (Street number and name)   (Apt. number)

   (City)   (State)   (ZIP Code)

3. Telephone number (include area code)

4. Student admission number

5. Social Security number

6. Date of birth

7. Country of birth

8. Country of citizenship

9. Passport issued by (country)

10. Passport expires on (date)

11. Date of intended departure

12. Has an immigrant visa petition ever been filed on your behalf?

   ☐ No   ☐ Yes (If yes, where was it filed?)

13. Have you ever applied for an immigrant visa or permanent residence in the U.S.?

   ☐ No   ☐ Yes (If yes, where did you apply?)

14. Have you been arrested or convicted of any criminal offense since entry into the U.S.?

   ☐ No   ☐ Yes (If yes, explain.)

15. Have you engaged in unauthorized employment while in student status?

   ☐ No   ☐ Yes (If yes, explain.)

B. This Section to be completed only by applicants for extension of stay.

1. Current means and source of support.

2. Reason for requesting extension of stay

C. This Section to be completed only if applying for extension of stay for your F-2 or M-2 dependents.

Name of dependent	Relationship	Country of birth	Date of birth	Passport issued by (country)	Passport expires on (date)

Block below for INS use only.

Microfilm index number	Initial Receipt	Resubmitted	Relocated		Completed		
			Received	Sent	Approved	Denied	Returned

138

Form I-538 (03/1/88) N

This Section to be completed only if an M-1 student applying for school transfer.

Date first granted M-1 status

2. Date (s) of absence from the U.S. since granted M-1 status

Reason you are requesting a transfer

This Section to be completed only if applying for permission to accept off-campus employment.

Date first granted F-1 status

2. Date (s) of absence from the U.S. during first year in F-1 status

Explain the financial changes that make it necessary for you to seek off-campus employment.

This Section to be completed only if applying for permission to engage in practical training.

Describe the proposed employment, giving beginning and ending dates and number of hours per week.

List all periods of perviously authorized employment for practical training.

A. Prior to completion of studies	B. Curricular or work/study	C. Post completion of studies

Signature of applicant
I certify, under penalty of purjury, that the information in this form is true and correct.

Signature   Date

Signature of person preparing form, if other than the applicant
I declare that this application was prepared by me at the request of the applicant and is based on all information of which I have any knowledge.

Signature   Date

Name (type or print)   Address

CERTIFICATION OF DESIGNATED SCHOOL OFFICIAL
(This section must be completed by the designated school official of the school the student is attending or was last authorized to attend.)

Name (Family in CAPS)   (First)   (Middle)   4. Level of education being sought

Student admission number   3. Date of birth   5. Student's major field of study

I hereby certify that:

☐ A.   The student named above;

  ☐ Is taking a full course of study at this school, and the expected date of completion is: _____

  ☐ Is taking less than a full course of study at this school because: _____

  ☐ Completed the course of study at this school on (date): _____

  ☐ Did not complete the course of study. Terminated attendance on (date): _____

☐ B.   The employment is for practical training in the student's field of study and, upon my information and belief, is not available in the country of the student's residence. The student has been in the educational program for at least 9 months and is eligible for the requested practical training in accordance with INS regulations at 8 CFR 214.2(f)(10).

☐ C.   Employment off-campus is due to unforeseen circumstances arising after entry. Acceptance of employment will not interfere with the student's carring a full course of study.

If application is for extension of stay or for permission to accept or continue off-campus employment, complete the following:

A. Student's cost for an academic term of (number of months, not to exceed 12). _____

B. Student's means of support estimated for the same period of time as in item A.

Tuition and fees $ _____	Personal funds of student $ _____
Living expenses $ _____	Family funds from abroad $ _____
Expenses of dependents $ _____	Funds from the school (specify type) $ _____
Other $ _____	Funds from other source (specify type) $ _____
	Employment, if applicable $ _____
TOTAL $ _____	TOTAL $ _____

Name and title of designated school official	Signature	Date	For Official Use Only Microfilm Index Number
Name of school	School file number (including suffix)	Telephone number	

I-538 (03/15/88) N

139

U.S. Department of Justice
Immigration and Naturalization Service

OMB #1115-009
Application to Extend/ChangeNonimmigrant Statu

START HERE - Please Type or Print

Part 1. Information about you.

Family Name	Given Name	Middle Initial

Address - In
Care of:

Street # and Name		Apt.#
City	State	
Zip Code		

Date of Birth (month/day/year)	Country of Birth
Social Security # (if any)	A# (if any)
Date of Last Arrival Into the U.S.	I-94#
Current Nonimmigrant Status	Expires on (month/day/year)

Part 2. Application Type.   (See instructions for fee.)

1. **I am applying for:** (check one)
   a. ☐ an extension of stay in my current status
   b. ☐ a change of status. The new status I am requesting is: _____
2. **Number of people included in this application:** (check one)
   a. ☐ I am the only applicant
   b. ☐ Members of my family are filing this application with me.
      The Total number of people included in this application is: ___
      (complete the supplement for each co-applicant)

Part 3. Processing information.

1. I/We request that my/our current or requested
   status be extended until (month/day/year) _____

2. Is this application based on an extension or change of status already granted to your spouse, child or parent?
   ☐ No   ☐ Yes (receipt # _____)

3. Is this application being filed based on a separate petition or application to give your spouse, child or parent an extension or change of status?
   ☐ No   ☐ Yes, filed with this application   ☐ Yes, filed previously and pending with INS

4. If you answered yes to question 3, give the petitioner or applicant name:

   If the application is pending with INS, also give the following information.

Office filed at_____ Filed on _____ (date)

Part 4. Additional information.

1. For applicant #1, provide passport information:

Country of issuance	Valid to: (month/day/year)

2. Foreign address:

Street # and Name		Apt#
City or Town	State or Province	
Country	Zip or Postal Code	

Form I-539 (Rev. 12-2-91)

140

FOR INS USE ONLY

Returned	Receipt
Date _____	
Resubmitted	
Date _____	
Reloc Sent	
Date _____	
Reloc Rec'd	
Date _____	
Date _____	

☐ Applicant Interviewed

☐ *Extension Granted*
   to (date):_____

☐ *Change of Status/Extension Granted*
New Class:_____ To (date):_____

If denied:
☐ Still within period of stay
☐ V/D to: _____
☐ S/D to:_____
☐ Place under docket control

Remarks

Action Block

To Be Completed by **Attorney** or **Representative**, if any
☐ Fill in box if G-28 is attached to represen the applicant
VOLAG#
ATTY State License #

Part 4. Additional Information. *(continued)*

3. Answer the following questions. If you answer yes to any question, explain on separate paper.	Yes	No
a. Are you, or any other person included in this application, an applicant for an immigrant visa or adjustment of status to permanent residence?		
b. Has an immigrant petition ever been filed for you, or for any other person included in this application?		
c. Have you, or any other person included in this application ever been arrested or convicted of any criminal offense since last entering the U.S.?		
d. Have you, or any other person included in this application done anything which violated the terms of the nonimmigrant status you now hold?		
e. Are you, or any other person included in this application, now in exclusion or deportation proceedings?		
f. Have you, or any other person included in this application, been employed in the U.S. since last admitted or granted an extension or change of status?		

If you answered YES to question 3f, give the following information on a separate paper: Name of person, name of employer, address of employer, weekly income, and whether specifically authorized by INS.

If you answered NO to question 3f, fully describe how you are supporting yourself on a separate paper. Include the source and the amount and basis for any income.

Part 5. Signature. *Read the information on penalties in the instructions before completing this section. You must file this application while in the United States.*

I certify under penalty of perjury under the laws of the United States of America that this application, and the evidence submitted with it, is all true and correct. I authorize the release of any information from my records which the Immigration and Naturalization Service needs to determine eligibility for the benefit I am seeking.

Signature	Print your name	Date

Please Note: If you do not completely fill out this form, or fail to submit required documents listed in the instructions, you cannot be found eligible for the requested document and this application will have to be denied.

Part 6. Signature of person preparing form if other than above. *(Sign below)*

I declare that I prepared this application at the request of the above person and it is based on all information of which I have knowledge.

Signature	Print Your Name	Date

Firm Name
and Address

(Please remember to enclose the mailing label with your application)

141

Form I-539 (Rev. 12-2-91)

Supplement-1

Attach to Form I-539 when more than one person is included in the petition or application. *(List each per* *separately. Do not include the person you named on the form).*

Family Name		Given Name	Middle Initial	Date of Birth (month/day/year)
Country of Birth		Social Security No.	A#	
IF IN THE U.S.	Date of Arrival *(month/day/year)*		I-94#	
	Current Nonimmigrant Status		Expires on *(month/day/year)*	
Country where passport issued		Expiration Date (month/day/year)		

Family Name		Given Name	Middle Initial	Date of Birth (month/day/year)
Country of Birth		Social Security No.	A#	
IF IN THE U.S.	Date of Arrival *(month/day/year)*		I-94#	
	Current Nonimmigrant Status:		Expires on *(month/day/year)*	
Country where passport issued		Expiration Date (month/day/year)		

Family Name		Given Name	Middle Initial	Date of Birth (month/day/year)
Country of Birth		Social Security No.	A#	
IF IN THE U.S.	Date of Arrival *(month/day/year)*		I-94#	
	Current Nonimmigrant Status:		Expires on *(month/day/year)*	
Country where passport issued		Expiration Date (month/day/year)		

Family Name		Given Name	Middle Initial	Date of Birth (month/day/year)
Country of Birth		Social Security No.	A#	
IF IN THE U.S.	Date of Arrival *(month/day/year)*		I-94#	
	Current Nonimmigrant Status:		Expires on *(month/day/year)*	
Country where passport issued		Expiration Date (month/day/year)		

Family Name		Given Name	Middle Initial	Date of Birth (month/day/year)
Country of Birth		Social Security No.	A#	
IF IN THE U.S.	Date of Arrival *(month/day/year)*		I-94#	
	Current Nonimmigrant Status:		Expires on *(month/day/year)*	
Country where passport issued		Expiration Date (month/day/year)		

U.S. Department of Justice
Immigration and Naturalization Service

OMB No. 1115-0145

Petition to Remove the Conditions on Residence

START HERE - Please Type or Print

Part 1. Information about you.

Family Name	Given Name	Middle Initial

Address - C/O:

Street Number and Name		Apt. #
City	State or Province	
Country	ZIP/Postal Code	

Date of Birth (month/day/year)	Country of Birth
Social Security #	A #

Conditional residence expires on (month/day/year)

Mailing address if different from residence C/O:

Street Number and Name		Apt. #
City	State or Province	
Country	ZIP/Postal Code	

Part 2. Basis for Eligibility (check one)

- [ ] My conditional residence is based on my marriage to a U.S. citizen or permanent resident, and we are filing this petition together.
- [ ] I am a child who entered as a conditional permanent resident and I am unable to be included in a Joint Petition to Remove the Conditional Basis of Alien's Permanent Residence (Form I-751) filed by my parent(s)

My conditional residence is based on my marriage to a U.S. citizen or permanent resident, but I am unable to file a joint petition and I request a waiver because: (check one)

- [ ] My spouse is deceased.
- [ ] I entered into the marriage in good faith, but the marriage was terminated through divorce/annulment.
- [ ] I am a conditional resident spouse who entered in to the marriage in good faith, or I am a conditional resident child, who has been battered or subjected to extreme mental cruelty by my citizen or permanent resident spouse or parent.
- [ ] The termination of my status and deportation from the United States would result in an extreme hardship.

Part 3. Additional information about you.

Other names used (including maiden name):	Telephone #
Date of Marriage	Place of Marriage

If your spouse is deceased, give the date of death (month/day/year)

Are you in deportation or exclusion proceedings?   [ ] Yes   [ ] No

Was a fee paid to anyone other than an attorney in connection with this petition?   [ ] Yes   [ ] No

Form I-751 (Rev. 12-4-91)   Continued on back.   143

FOR INS USE ONLY

Returned	Receipt

Resubmitted

Reloc Sent

Reloc Rec'd

[ ] Applicant Interviewed

Remarks

Action

To Be Completed by Attorney or Representative, if any

[ ] Fill in box if G-28 is attached to represent the applicant

VOLAG#

ATTY State License #

Part 3. Additional Information about you. (con't)

Since becoming a conditional resident, have you ever been arrested, cited, charged, indicted, convicted, fined or imprisoned for breaking or violating any law or ordinance (excluding traffic regulations), or committed any crime for which you were not arrested?   ☐ Yes ☐ No

If you are married, is this a different marriage than the one through which conditional residence status was obtained?   ☐ Yes ☐ No

Have you resided at any other address since you became a permanent resident?   ☐ Yes ☐ No *(If yes, attach a list of all addresses and dates.)*

Is your spouse currently serving employed by the U. S. government and serving outside the U.S.?   ☐ Yes ☐ No

Part 4. Information about the spouse or parent through whom you gained your conditional residence

Family Name	Given Name	Middle Initial	Phone Number ( )

Address

Date of Birth *(month/day/year)*	Social Security #	A#

Part 5. Information about your children. *List _all_ your children.   Attach another sheet if necessary*

	Name	Date of Birth *(month/day/year)*	If in U.S., give A#, current immigration status and U.S. Address	Living with you?
1				☐ Yes ☐ No
2				☐ Yes ☐ No
3				☐ Yes ☐ No
4				☐ Yes ☐ No

Part 6. Complete if you are requesting a waiver of the joint filing petition requirement based on extreme mental cruelty

~~SAMPLE~~

Evaluator's ID Number: State: [ ] Number: [ ]		Expires on *(month/day/year)*	Occupation
Last Name	First Name		Address

Part 7. Signature. *Read the information on penalties in the instructions before completing this section. If you checked block "a" in Part 2 your spouse must also sign below.*

I certify, under penalty of perjury under the laws of the United States of America, that this petition, and the evidence submitted with it, is all true and correct. conditional residence was based on a marriage, I further certify that the marriage was entered into in accordance with the laws of the place where the marriage took place, and was not for the purpose of procuring an immigration benefit. I also authorize the release of any information from my records which the Immigration and Naturalization Service needs to determine eligibility for the benefit being sought.

Signature	Print Name	Date
Signature of Spouse	Print Name	Date

Please note: If you do not completely fill out this form, or fail to submit any required documents listed in the instructions, then you cannot be found eligible for the requested benefit, and this petition may be denied.

Part 8. Signature of person preparing form if other than above.

I declare that I prepared this petition at the request of the above person and it is based on all information of which I have knowledge.

Signature	Print Name	Date

Firm Name and Address

Form I-751 (Rev. 12-4-91)   ★ GPO : 1992 0 - 316-46

U.S. Department of Justice
Immigration and Naturalization Service

OMB # 1115-0163

Application for Employment Authorization

Do Not Write In This Block

Remarks	Action Stamp	Fee Stamp
A#		

Applicant is filing under 274a.12_____

☐ Application Approved. Employment Authorized / Extended (Circle One) _____ (Date).

until _____ (Date).

Subject to the following conditions: _____

☐ Application Denied.
  ☐ Failed to establish eligibility under 8 CFR 274a.12 (a) or (c).
  ☐ Failed to establish economic necessity as required in 8 CFR 274a.12(c) (14), (18) and 8 CFR 214.2(f)

I am applying for: ☐ Permission to accept employment
     ☐ Replacement (of lost employment authorization document).
     ☐ Extension of my permission to accept employment (attach previous employment authorization document).

1. Name (Family Name in CAPS) (First) (Middle)

2. Other Names Used (Include Maiden Name)

3. Address in the United States (Number and Street) (Apt. Number)

  (Town or City) (State/Country) (ZIP Code)

4. Country of Citizenship/Nationality

5. Place of Birth (Town or City) (State/Province) (Country)

6. Date of Birth (Month/Day/Year)   7. Sex   ☐ Male ☐ Female

8. Marital Status   ☐ Married ☐ Single ☐ Widowed ☐ Divorced

9. Social Security Number (Include all Numbers you have ever used)

10. Alien Registration Number (A-Number) or I-94 Number (if any)

11. Have you ever before applied for employment authorization from INS?
  ☐ Yes (If yes, complete below)   ☐ No

  Which INS Office?   Date(s)

  Results (Granted or Denied - attach all documentation)

12. Date of Last Entry into the U.S. (Month/Day/Year)

13. Place of Last Entry into the U.S.

14. Manner of Last Entry (Visitor, Student, etc.)

15. Current Immigration Status (Visitor, Student, etc.)

16. Go to Part 2 of the instructions, Eligibility Categories. In the space below, place the letter and number of the category you selected from the instructions (For example, (a)(8), (c)(17)(iii),etc.).

Eligibility under 8 CFR 274a.12

(   ) (   ) (   )

Certification

Your Certification: I certify, under penalty of perjury under the laws of the United States of America, that the foregoing is true and correct. Furthermore, I authorize the release of any information which the Immigration and Naturalization Service needs to determine eligibility for the benefit I am seeking. I have read the instructions in Part 2 and have identified the appropriate eligibility category in Block 16.

Signature	Telephone Number	Date

Signature of Person Preparing Form If Other Than Above: I declare that this document was prepared by me at the request of the applicant and is based on all information of which I have any knowledge.

Print Name	Address	Signature	Date

Initial receipt	Resubmitted	Relocated		Completed		
		Rec'd	Sent	Approved	Denied	Returned

Form I-765 (Rev. 04/25/95) N Page 7

PLEASE DO NOT STAPLE THIS FORM

ASSURE THAT IMPRESSIONS ON
ALL COPIES ARE CLEAR

APPROVED OMB 3116-0006 EXP. 10/31/92
*Estimated Burden Hours: 15 mins. (See page 4)

United States Information Agency
EXCHANGE VISITOR FACILITATIVE STAFF GC/V
CERTIFICATE OF ELIGIBILITY FOR EXCHANGE VISITOR (J-1) STATUS

D

( ) Male
( ) Female

1 _____
   (FAMILY NAME OF EXCHANGE VISITOR)   (FIRST NAME)   (MIDDLE NAME)

born ____ ____ ____ in _____
   (Mo.) (Day) (Yr.)   (City)   (Country)

a citizen of _____ _____ a legal permanent resident of _____
   (Country)   (Code)

_____ _____, whose position in that country is _____
   (Country)   (Code)

_____ _____
   (Pos. Code)

U.S. address _____

THE PURPOSE OF THIS FORM IS TO:

1 ( ) Begin a new program ( ) Accompanied by
      _____ immediate family members

2 ( ) Extend an on-going program.

3 ( ) Transfer to a different program.

4 ( ) Replace a lost form.

5 ( ) Permit visitor's immediate family
      (_____ members) to enter U.S. separately.

2. will be sponsored by _____
   _____ to participate in Exchange Visitor Program No ____ - ____ - _____, which is still valid and is officially described as follows:

3. This form covers the period from ____ ____ ____ to ____ ____ ____ Students are permitted to travel abroad & maintain status (e.g. obtain a new visa)
   (Mo.) (Day) (Yr.)   (Mo.) (Day) (Yr.)
   under duration of the program as indicated by the dates on this from.
   If this form is for family travel or replaces a lost form, the expiration date on the exchange visitor's I-94 is _____

4. The category of this visitor is 1 ( ) Student, 2 ( ) Trainee, 3 ( ) Teacher, 4 ( ) Professor, Research Scholar or Specialist, 5 ( ) International Visitor, 6 ( ) Medical
   Trainee, 7 ( ) Alien employee of the USIA. The Specific field of study, research, training or professional activity is_____ verbally described as follows:
   (Subfield Code)

5. During the period covered by this form, it is estimated that the following financial support (in U.S. $) will be provided to this exchange visitor by:

   a. ( ) The Program Sponsor in Item 2 above $ _____

   This Program Sponsor has [ ] has not [ ] (check one) received funding for international exchange from one or more U.S. Government
   Agency(ies) to support this exchange visitor. If any U.S. Government Agency(ies) provided funding, indicate the Agency(ies) by code ___ ___ ___.

   Financial support from organizations other than the sponsor will be provided by one or more of the following:

   b1. ( ) U.S. Government Agency(ies): _____ (Agency Code), $ _____; b2 _____ (Agency Code), $ _____
   c1. ( ) International Organization(s): _____ (Int. Org. Code), $ _____; c2 _____ (Int. Org. Code), $ _____
   d. ( ) The Exchange Visitor's Government $ _____
   e. ( ) The binational Commission of the visitor's Country $ _____
   f. ( ) All other organizations providing support $ _____
   g. ( ) Personal funds $ _____

   (If necessary, use above spaces
   for funding by multiple U.S.
   Agencies or Intl. Organizations)

6. I.N.S. USE

7. _____
   (Name of Official Preparing Form)   (Title)

   _____
   (Address)

   _____
   (Signature of Responsible Officer or Alternate R.O.)   (Date)

PRELIMINARY ENDORSEMENT OF CONSULAR OR IMMIGRATION OFFICER
REGARDING SECTION 212 (e) OF THE I.N.S.

I. (Name) _____
   (Title) _____

have determined that this alien in the above program
1. ( ) is not subject to the two year residence requirement
2. ( ) is subject based on: — A. ( ) government financing and/or
                              B. ( ) the Exchange visitor skills list and/or
                              C. ( ) PL 94 484 as amended
The United States Information Agency reserves the right to make the final determination.

_____
(Signature of Officer)   (Date)

8. STATEMENT OF RESPONSIBLE OFFICER FOR RELEASING
   SPONSOR (FOR TRANSFER OF PROGRAM)

Date_____, Transfer of this exchange visitor from program No. _____ sponsored by _____ to the program specified in item (2) is necessary or
highly desirable and is in conformity with the objectives of the Mutual Educational and Cultural
Exchange Act of 1961.

_____
(Signature of Officer)   (Date)

START HERE - Please Type or Print

Part 1. Information about you.

Family Name	Given Name	Middle Initial

U.S. **Mailing Address** - Care of

Street Number and Name	Apt. #

City	County

State	ZIP Code

Date of Birth (month/day/year)	Country of Birth

Social Security #	A #

Part 2. Basis for Eligibility *(check one)*.

- ☐ I have been a permanent resident for at least five (5) years.
- ☐ I have been a permanent resident for at least three (3) years and have been married to a United States Citizen for those three years.
- ☐ I am a permanent resident child of United States citizen parent(s).
- ☐ I am applying on the basis of qualifying military service in the Armed Forces of the U.S. and have attached completed Forms N-426 and G-325B.
- ☐ Other. (Please specify section of law) _____

Part 3. Additional information about you.

Date you became a permanent resident (month/day/year)	Port admitted with an immigrant visa or INS Office where granted adjustment of status

Citizenship

Name on alien registration card (if different than in Part 1)

Other names used since you became a permanent resident (including maiden name)

☐ Male ☐ Female	Height	Marital Status: ☐ Single ☐ Married	☐ Divorced ☐ Widowed

Can you speak, read and write English ?   ☐ No ☐ Yes.

Absences from the U.S.:

Have you been absent from the U.S. since becoming a permanent resident?   ☐ No ☐ Yes.

If you answered "**Yes**", complete the following. Begin with your most recent absence. If you need more room to explain the reason for an absence or to list more trips, continue on separate paper.

Date left U.S.	Date returned	Did absence last 6 months or more?	Destination	Reason for trip
		☐ Yes ☐ No		
		☐ Yes ☐ No		
		☐ Yes ☐ No		
		☐ Yes ☐ No		
		☐ Yes ☐ No		
		☐ Yes ☐ No		

Form N-400 (Rev. 07/17/91)N

FOR INS USE ONLY

Returned	Receipt

Resubmitted

Reloc Sent

Reloc Rec'd

☐ Applicant Interviewed

At interview
☐ request naturalization ceremony at court

Remarks

Action

To Be Completed by
Attorney or ***Representative***, if any

☐ Fill in box if G-28 is attached to represent the applicant

VOLAG#

ATTY State License #

Part 4. Information about your residences and employment.

A. List your addresses during the last five (5) years or since you became a permanent resident, whichever is less. Begin with your current address. If you n[eed] more space, continue on separate paper:

Street Number and Name, City, State, Country, and Zip Code	Dates (month/day/year)	
	From	To

B. List your employers during the last five (5) years. List your present or most recent employer first. If none, write "None". If you need more space, conti[nue] on separate paper.

Employer's Name	Employer's Address	Dates Employed (month/day/year)		Occupation/position
	Street Name and Number - City, State and ZIP Code	From	To	

Part 5. Information about your marital history.

A. Total number of times you have been married _____ . If you are now married, complete the following regarding your husband or wife.

Family name	Given name	Middle initial
Address		
Date of birth (month/day/year)	Country of birth	Citizenship
Social Security #	A# (if applicable)	Immigration status (If not a U.S. citizen)

Naturalization (If applicable)
(month/day/year)   Place   (City, State)

If you have ever previously been married or if your current spouse has been previously married, please provide the following on separate paper: Name of pr[ior] spouse, date of marriage, date marriage ended, how marriage ended and immigration status of prior spouse.

Part 6. Information about your children.

B. Total Number of Children _____ . Complete the following information for each of your children. If the child lives with you, state "with me" in [the] address column; otherwise give city/state/country of child's current residence. If deceased, write "deceased" in the address column. If you need m[ore] space, continue on separate paper.

Full name of child	Date of birth	Country of birth	Citizenship	A - Number	Address

Form N-400 (Rev. 07/17/91)N   *Continued on next page*

148

art 7. Additional eligibility factors.

ase answer each of the following questions. If your answer is "**Yes**", explain on a separate paper.

Are you now, or have you ever been a member of, or in any way connected or associated with the Communist Party, or ever knowingly aided or supported the Communist Party directly, or indirectly through another organization, group or person, or ever advocated, taught, believed in, or knowingly supported or furthered the interests of communism? ☐ Yes ☐ No

During the period March 23, 1933 to May 8, 1945, did you serve in, or were you in any way affiliated with, either directly or indirectly, any military unit, paramilitary unit, police unit, self-defence unit, vigilante unit, citizen unit of the Nazi party or SS, government agency or office, extermination camp, concentration camp, prisoner of war camp, prison, labor camp, detention camp or transit camp, under the control or affiliated with:

    a. The Nazi Government of Germany? ☐ Yes ☐ No

    b. Any government in any area occupied by, allied with, or established with the assistance or cooperation of, the Nazi Government of Germany? ☐ Yes ☐ No

Have you at any time, anywhere, ever ordered, incited, assisted, or otherwise participated in the persecution of any person because of race, religion, national origin, or political opinion? ☐ Yes ☐ No

Have you ever left the United States to avoid being drafted into the U.S. Armed Forces? ☐ Yes ☐ No

Have you ever failed to comply with Selective Service laws? ☐ Yes ☐ No

If you have registered under the Selective Service laws, complete the following information:

    Selective Service Number:_____ Date Registered:_____

If you registered before 1978, also provide the following:

    Local Board Number:_____ Classification:_____

Did you ever apply for exemption from military service because of alienage, conscientious objections or other reasons? ☐ Yes ☐ No

Have you ever deserted from the military, air or naval forces of the United States? ☐ Yes ☐ No

Since becoming a permanent resident , have you ever failed to file a federal income tax return? ☐ Yes ☐ No

Since becoming a permanent resident , have you filed a federal income tax return as a nonresident or failed to file a federal return because you considered yourself to be a nonresident? ☐ Yes ☐ No

Are deportation proceedings pending against you, or have you ever been deported, or ordered deported, or have you ever applied for suspension of deportation? ☐ Yes ☐ No

Have you ever claimed in writing, or in any way to be a United States citizen? ☐ Yes ☐ No

Have you ever:

    a. been a habitual drunkard? ☐ Yes ☐ No

    b. advocated or practiced polygamy? ☐ Yes ☐ No

    c. been a prostitute or procured anyone for prostitution? ☐ Yes ☐ No

    d. knowingly and for gain helped any alien to enter the U.S. illegally? ☐ Yes ☐ No

    e. been an illicit trafficker in narcotic drugs or marijuana? ☐ Yes ☐ No

    f. received income from illegal gambling? ☐ Yes ☐ No

g. given false testimony for the purpose of obtaining any immigration benefit? ☐ Yes ☐ No

Have you ever been declared legally incompetent or have you ever been confined as a patient in a mental institution? ☐ Yes ☐ No

Were you born with, or have you acquired in same way, any title or order of nobility in any foreign State? ☐ Yes ☐ No

Have you ever:

    a. knowingly committed any crime for which you have not been arrested? ☐ Yes ☐ No

    b. been arrested, cited, charged, indicted, convicted, fined or imprisoned for breaking or violating any law or ordinance excluding traffic regulations? ☐ Yes ☐ No

u answer yes to 15 , in your explanation give the following information for each incident or occurrence the **city, state,** and try, where the offense took place, the **date** and **nature** of the offense, and the **outcome** or **disposition** of the case).

Part 8. Allegiance to the U.S.

f your answer to any of the following questions is "**NO**", attach a full explanation:

    1. Do you believe in the Constitution and form of government of the U.S.? ☐ Yes ☐ No

    2. Are you willing to take the full Oath of Allegiance to the U.S.? (see instructions) ☐ Yes ☐ No

    3. If the law requires it, are you willing to bear arms on behalf of the U.S.? ☐ Yes ☐ No

    4. If the law requires it, are you willing to perform noncombatant services in the Armed Forces of the U.S.? ☐ Yes ☐ No

    5. If the law requires it, are you willing to perform work of national importance under civilian direction? ☐ Yes   No

Part 9. Memberships and organizations.

A. List your present and past membership in or affiliation with every organization, association, fund, foundation, party, club, society, or similar group in United States or in any other place. Include any military service in this part. If none, write "none". Include the name of organization, location, dates membership and the nature of the organization. If additional space is needed, use separate paper.

_____
_____
_____
_____

Part 10. Complete only if you checked block " C " in Part 2.

How many of your parents are U.S. citizens?   ☐ One   ☐ Both   (Give the following about one U.S. citizen parent:)

Family Name	Given Name	Middle Name

Address

Basis for citizenship: ☐ Birth ☐ Naturalization Cert. No.	Relationship to you (check one): ☐ natural parent ☐ adoptive parent ☐ parent of child legitimated after birth

If adopted or legitimated after birth, give date of adoption or, legitimation: _(month/day/year)_ _____

Does this parent have legal custody of you?   ☐ Yes   ☐ No

(Attach a copy of relating evidence to establish that you are the child of this U.S. citizen and evidence of this parent's citizenship.)

Part 11. Signature. _(Read the information on penalties in the instructions before completing this section)._

I certify or, if outside the United States, I swear or affirm, under penalty of perjury under the laws of the United States of America that this application, and the evidence submitted with it, is all true and correct. I authorize the release of any information from my records which the Immigration and Naturalization Service needs to determine eligibility for the benefit I am seeking.

Signature _____   Date _____

Please Note: _If you do not completely fill out this form, or fail to submit required documents listed in the instructions, you may not be found eligible for naturalization and this application may be denied._

Part 12. Signature of person preparing form if other than above. _(Sign below)_

I declare that I prepared this application at the request of the above person and it is based on all information of which I have knowledge.

Signature _____   **Print Your Name** _____   Date _____

Firm Name
and Address

DO NOT COMPLETE THE FOLLOWING UNTIL INSTRUCTED TO DO SO AT THE INTERVIEW

I swear that I know the contents of this application, and supplemental pages 1 through_____ , that the corrections , numbered 1 through_____ , were made at my request, and that this amended application, is true to the best of my knowledge and belief.

Subscribed and sworn to before me by the applicant.

_____
(Examiner's Signature)   Date

_____
(Complete and true signature of applicant)

PLEASE TYPE OR PRINT YOUR ANSWERS IN THE SPACE PROVIDED BELOW EACH ITEM.

1. SURNAMES OR FAMILY NAMES (*Exactly as in Passport*)

2. FIRST NAME AND MIDDLE NAME (*Exactly as in Passport*)

3. OTHER NAMES (*Maiden, Religious, Professional, Aliases*)

4. DATE OF BIRTH (*Day, Month, Year*) | 8. PASSPORT NUMBER

5. PLACE OF BIRTH
City, Province | Country | DATE PASSPORT ISSUED (*Day, Month, Year*)

6. NATIONALITY | 7. SEX ☐ MALE ☐ FEMALE | DATE PASSPORT EXPIRES (*Day, Month, Year*)

9. HOME ADDRESS (*Include apartment no., street, city, province, and postal zone*)

10. NAME AND STREET ADDRESS OF PRESENT EMPLOYER OR SCHOOL (*Postal box number unacceptable*)

11. HOME TELEPHONE NO. | 12. BUSINESS TELEPHONE NO.

13. COLOR OF HAIR | 14. COLOR OF EYES | 15. COMPLEXION

16. HEIGHT | 17. MARKS OF IDENTIFICATION

18. MARITAL STATUS
☐ Married ☐ Single ☐ Widowed ☐ Divorced ☐ Separated
If married, give name and nationality of spouse.

19. NAMES AND RELATIONSHIPS OF PERSONS TRAVELING WITH YOU (NOTE: A separate application must be made for a visa for each traveler, regardless of age.)

20. HAVE YOU EVER APPLIED FOR A U.S. VISA BEFORE, WHETHER IMMIGRANT OR NONIMMIGRANT?
☐ No
☐ Yes Where? _____
When? _____ Type of visa? _____
☐ Visa was issued ☐ Visa was refused

21. HAS YOUR U.S. VISA EVER BEEN CANCELED?
☐ No
☐ Yes Where? _____
When? _____ By whom? _____

22. Bearers of visitors visas may generally not work or study in the U.S.
DO YOU INTEND TO WORK IN THE U.S.? ☐ No ☐ Yes
If YES, explain.

23. DO YOU INTEND TO STUDY IN THE U.S.? ☐ No ☐ Yes
If YES, write name and address of school as it appears on form I-20.

DO NOT WRITE IN THIS SPACE

B-1/B-2 MAX   B-1 MAX   B-2 MAX

OTHER_____MAX
Visa Classification

MULT OR _____
Number Applications

MONTHS_____
Validity

L.O. CHECKED_____

ISSUED/REFUSED
ON _____ BY _____

UNDER SEC. _____ INA

REFUSAL REVIEWED BY _____

24. PRESENT OCCUPATION (*If retired, state last occupation*)

25. WHO WILL FURNISH FINANCIAL SUPPORT, INCLUDING TICKETS?

26. AT WHAT ADDRESS WILL YOU STAY IN THE U.S.A.?

27. WHAT IS THE PURPOSE OF YOUR TRIP?

28. WHEN DO YOU INTEND TO ARRIVE IN THE U.S.A.?

29. HOW LONG DO YOU PLAN TO STAY IN THE U.S.A.?

30. HAVE YOU EVER BEEN IN THE U.S.A.?
☐ No
☐ Yes When? _____
For how long? _____

NONIMMIGRANT VISA APPLICATION

COMPLETE ALL QUESTIONS ON REVERSE OF FORM

OPTIONAL FORM 156 (Rev. 6-93) Page 1
Department of State

50156-108
PREVIOUS EDITIONS OBSOLETE

NSN 7540-00-139-0053

SAMPLE

31. (a) HAVE YOU OR ANYONE ACTING FOR YOU EVER INDICATED TO A U.S. CONSULAR OR IMMIGRATION EMPLOYEE A DESIRE TO IMMIGRATE TO THE U.S.? (b) HAS ANYONE EVER FILED AN IMMIGRANT VISA PETITION ON YOUR BEHALF? (c) HAS LABOR CERTIFICATION FOR EMPLOYMENT IN THE U.S. EVER BEEN REQUESTED BY YOU OR ON YOUR BEHALF?

(a) ☐ No ☐ Yes   (b) ☐ No ☐ Yes   (c) ☐ No ☐ Yes

32. ARE ANY OF THE FOLLOWING IN THE U.S.? (If YES, circle appropriate relationship and indicate that person's status in the U.S., i.e. studying, working, U.S. permanent resident, U.S. citizen, etc.)

HUSBAND/WIFE _____ FIANCE/FIANCEE _____ BROTHER/SISTER _____

FATHER/MOTHER _____ SON/DAUGHTER _____

33. PLEASE LIST THE COUNTRIES WHERE YOU HAVE LIVED FOR MORE THAN 6 MONTHS DURING THE PAST 5 YEARS. BEGIN WITH YOUR PRESENT RESIDENCE.

Countries	Cities	Approximate Dates

34. IMPORTANT: ALL APPLICANTS MUST READ AND CHECK THE APPROPRIATE BOX FOR EACH ITEM:

A visa may not be issued to persons who are within specific categories defined by law as inadmissible to the United States (except when a waiver is obtained in advance). Are any of the following applicable to you?

- Have you ever been afflicted with a communicable disease of public health significance, a dangerous physical or mental disorder, or been a drug abuser or addict? . . . . ☐ Yes ☐ No

- Have you ever been arrested or convicted for any offense or crime, even though subject of a pardon, amnesty, or other such legal action? . . . . ☐ Yes ☐ No

- Have you ever been a controlled substance (drug) trafficker, or a prostitute or procurer? . . . . . ☐ Yes ☐ No

- Have you ever sought to obtain or assist others to obtain a visa, entry into the U.S., or any U.S. Immigration benefit by fraud or willful misrepresentation? . . . . ☐ Yes ☐ No

- Were you deported from the U.S.A. within the last 5 years? . . . . ☐ Yes ☐ No

- Do you seek to enter the United States to engage in export control violations, subversive or terrorist activities, or any unlawful purpose? . . . . ☐ Yes ☐ No

- Have you ever ordered, incited, assisted, or otherwise participated in the persecution of any person because of race, religion, national origin, or political opinion under the control, direct or indirect, of the Nazi Government of Germany, or of the government of any area occupied by, or allied with, the Nazi Government of Germany; or have you ever participated in genocide? . . . . . ☐ Yes ☐ No

A YES answer does not automatically signify ineligibility for a visa but if you answered YES to any of the above, or if you have any question in this regard, personal appearance at this office is recommended. If appearance is not possible at this time, attach a statement of facts in your case to this application.

35. I certify that I have read and understood all the questions set forth in this application and the answers I have furnished on this form are true and correct to the best of my knowledge and belief. I understand that any false or misleading statement may result in the permanent refusal of a visa or denial of entry into the United States. I understand that possession of a visa does not entitle the bearer to enter the United States of America upon arrival at port of entry if he or she is found inadmissible.

DATE OF APPLICATION _____

APPLICANT'S SIGNATURE _____

If this application has been prepared by a travel agency or another person on your behalf, the agent should indicate name and address of agency or person with appropriate signature of individual preparing form.

SIGNATURE OF PERSON PREPARING FORM _____
(If other than applicant)

DO NOT WRITE IN THIS SPACE

37 mm x 37 mm

—— PHOTO ——

Glue or staple
photo here

OPTIONAL FORM 156 (Rev. 6-93) PAGE 2
Department of State

CUT ALONG DOTTED LINE

U.S. DEPARTMENT OF LABOR
Employment and Training Administration

APPLICATION
FOR
ALIEN EMPLOYMENT CERTIFICATION

IMPORTANT: READ CAREFULLY BEFORE COMPLETING THIS FORM

PRINT legibly in ink or use a typewriter. If you need more space to answer questions on this form, use a separate sheet. Identify each answer with the number of the corresponding question. SIGN AND DATE each sheet in original signature.

To knowingly furnish any false information in the preparation of this form and any supplement thereto or to aid, abet, or counsel another to do so is a felony punishable by $10,000 fine or 5 years in the penitentiary, or both (18 U.S.C. 1001).

PART A. OFFER OF EMPLOYMENT

1. Name of Alien *(Family name in capital letter, First, Middle, Maiden)*

2. Present Address of Alien *(Number, Street, City and Town, State ZIP Code or Province, Country)*

3. Type of Visa *(If in U.S.)*

The following information is submitted as evidence of an offer of employment.

4. Name of Employer *(Full name of organization)*

5. Telephone *(Area Code and Number)*

6. Address *(Number, Street, City or Town, Country, State, ZIP Code)*

7. Address Where Alien Will Work *(if different from item 6)*

8. Nature of Employer's Business Activity

9. Name of Job Title

10. Total Hours Per Week
   a. Basic
   b. Overtime

11. Work Schedule *(Hourly)*
   a.m.
   p.m.

12. Rate of Pay
   a. Basic $ _____ per ....
   b. Overtime $ _____ per hour

13. Describe Fully the Job to be Performed *(Duties)*

14. State in detail the MINIMUM education, training, and experience for a worker to perform satisfactorily the job duties described in Item 13 above.

15. Other Special Requirements

EDUCATION *(Enter number of years)*	Grade School	High School	College	College Degree Required *(specify)*
				Major Field of Study

TRAINING	No. Yrs.	No. Mos.	Type of Training

EXPERIENCE	Job Offered		Related Occupation		Related Occupation *(specify)*
	Yrs.	Mos.	Yrs.	Mos.	

16. Occupational Title of Person Who Will Be Alien's Immediate Supervisor ➤

17. Number of Employees Alien will Supervise ➤

◄ ENDORSEMENTS *(Make no entry in section - for government use only)*

Date Forms Received	
L.O.	S.O.
R.O.	N.O.
Ind. Code	Occ. Code
Occ. Title	

Replaces MA 7-50A, B and C (Apr. 1970 edition) which is obsolete.

ETA 750 (Oct. 1979)

18. COMPLETE ITEMS ONLY IF JOB IS TEMPORARY			19. IF JOB IS UNIONIZED *(Complete)*	
a. No. of Openings To Be Filled By Aliens Under Job Offer	b. Exact Dates You Expect To Employ Alien		a. Number of Local	b. Name of Local
	From	To		
				c. City and State

20. STATEMENT FOR LIVE-AT-WORK JOB OFFERS *(Complete for Private Household Job ONLY)*

a. Description of Residence		b. No. Persons Residing at Place of Employment				c. Will free board and private room not shared with any-one be provided?	*("X" one)*
("X" one)	Number of Rooms	Adults		Children	Ages		☐ YES ☐ NO
☐ House			BOYS				
☐ Apartment			GIRLS				

21. DESCRIBE EFFORTS TO RECRUIT U.S. WORKERS AND THE RESULTS. *(Specify Sources of Recruitment by Name)*

22. Applications require various types of documentation. Please read PART II of the instructions to assure that appropriate supporting documentation is included with your application.

23. EMPLOYER CERTIFICATIONS

By virtue of my signature below, I HEREBY CERTIFY the following conditions of employment.

a. I have enough funds available to pay the wage or salary offered the alien.

b. The wage offered equals or exceeds the prevailing wage and I guarantee that, if a labor certification is granted, the wage paid to the alien when the alien begins work will equal or exceed the prevailing wage which is applicable at the time the alien begins work.

c. The wage offered is not based on commissions, bonuses, or other incentives, unless I guarantee a wage paid on a weekly, bi-weekly or monthly basis.

d. I will be able to place the alien on the payroll on or before the date of the alien's proposed entrance into the United States.

e. The job opportunity does not involve unlawful discrimination by race, creed, color, national origin, age, sex, religion, handicap, or citizenship.

f. The job opportunity is not:

(1) Vacant because the former occupant is on strike or is being locked out in the course of a labor dispute involving a work stoppage.

(2) At issue in a labor dispute involving a work stoppage.

g. The job opportunity's terms, conditions and occupational environment are not contrary to Federal, State or local law.

h. The job opportunity has been and is clearly open to any qualified U.S. worker.

24. DECLARATIONS

DECLARATION OF EMPLOYER ➤ *Pursuant to 28 U.S.C. 1746, I declare under penalty of perjury the foregoing is true and correct.*

SIGNATURE	DATE
NAME *(Type or Print)*	TITLE

AUTHORIZATION OF AGENT OF EMPLOYER ➤ *I HEREBY DESIGNATE the agent below to represent me for the purposes of labor certification and I TAKE FULL RESPONSIBILITY for accuracy of any representations made by my agent.*

SIGNATURE OF EMPLOYER	DATE
NAME OF AGENT *(Type or Print)*	ADDRESS OF AGENT *(Number, Street, City, State, ZIP Code)*

PART B. STATEMENT OF QUALIFICATIONS OF ALIEN

FOR ADVICE CONCERNING REQUIREMENTS FOR ALIEN EMPLOYMENT CERTIFICATION: *If alien is in the U.S., contact nearest office of Immigration and Naturalization Service. If alien is outside U.S., contact nearest U.S. Consulate.*

IMPORTANT: READ ATTACHED INSTRUCTIONS BEFORE COMPLETING THIS FORM.

Print legibly in ink or use a typewriter. If you need more space to fully answer any questions on this form, use a separate sheet. Identify each answer with the number of the corresponding question. Sign and date each sheet.

1. Name of Alien *(Family name in capital letters)*	First name	Middle name	Maiden name

2. Present Address *(No., Street, City or Town, State or Province and ZIP Code*	Country	3. Type of Visa *(If in U.S.)*

4. Alien's Birthdate *(Month, Day, Year)*	5. Birthplace *(City or Town, State or Province)*	Country	6. Present Nationality or Citizenship *(Country)*

7. Address in United States Where Alien Will Reside

8. Name and Address of Prospective Employer If Alien has Job offer in U.S.	9. Occupation in which Alien is Seeking Work

10. "X" the appropriate box below and furnish the information required for the box marked

	City in Foreign Country	Foreign Country
a. ☐ Alien will apply for a visa abroad at the American Consulate in →		
	City	State
b. ☐ Alien is in the United States and will apply for adjustment of status to that of a lawful permanent resident in the office of the Immigration and Naturalization Service at →		

11. Names and Addresses of Schools, Colleges and Universities Attended *(Include trade or vocational training facilities)*	Field of Study	FROM Month	FROM Year	TO Month	TO Year	Degrees or Certificates Received

SPECIAL QUALIFICATIONS AND SKILLS

12. Additional Qualifications and Skills Alien Possesses and Proficiency in the use of Tools, Machines or Equipment Which Would Help Establish If Alien Meets Requirements for Occupation in Item 9.

13. List Licenses *(Professional, journeyman, etc.)*

14. List Documents Attached Which are Submitted as Evidence that Alien Possesses the Education, Training, Experience, and Abilities Represented

Endorsements	DATE REC. DOL
	O.T. & C.
(Make no entry in this section — FOR Government Agency USE ONLY)	

(Items continued on next page)

155

15. WORK EXPERIENCE. List all jobs held during past three (3) years. Also, list any other jobs related to the occupation for which the alien is seeking certification as indicated in item 9

a. NAME AND ADDRESS OF EMPLOYER

NAME OF JOB	DATE STARTED Month Year	DATE LEFT Month Year	KIND OF BUSINESS

DESCRIBE IN DETAILS THE DUTIES PERFORMED, INCLUDING THE USE OF TOOLS, MACHINES, OR EQUIPMENT	NO. OF HOURS PER WEEK

b. NAME AND ADDRESS OF EMPLOYER

NAME OF JOB	DATE STARTED Month Year	DATE LEFT Month Year	KIND OF BUSINESS

DESCRIBE IN DETAIL THE DUTIES PERFORMED, INCLUDING THE USE OF TOOLS, MACHINES, OR EQUIPMENT	NO. OF HOURS PER WEEK

c. NAME AND ADDRESS OF EMPLOYER

NAME OF JOB	DATE STARTED Month Year	DATE LEFT Month Year	KIND OF BUSINESS

DESCRIBE IN DETAIL THE DUTIES PERFORMED, INCLUDING THE USE OF TOOLS, MACHINES, OR EQUIPMENT	NO. OF HOURS PER WEEK

SAMPLE

16. DECLARATIONS

DECLARATION OF ALIEN ► ► Pursuant to 28 U.S.C. 1746, I declare under penalty of perjury the foregoing is true and correct.

SIGNATURE OF ALIEN	DATE

AUTHORIZATION OF AGENT OF ALIEN ► ► I hereby designate the agent below to represent me for the purposes of labor certification and I take full responsibility for accuracy of any representations made by my agent.

SIGNATURE OF ALIEN	DATE

NAME OF AGENT (Type or print)	ADDRESS OF AGENT (No., Street, City, State, ZIP Code)

156

Labor Condition Application for H-1B Nonimmigrants

U.S. Department of Labor
Employment and Training Administration
U.S. Employment Service

OMB Approval No.: 1205-0310
Expiration Date: 11-30-97

1. Full Legal Name of Employer	5. Employer's Address (No., Street, City, State, and ZIP Code)
2. Federal Employer I.D. Number	
3. Employer's Telephone No. ( )	6. Address Where Documentation is Kept (If different than item 5)
4. Employer's FAX No. ( )	

7. OCCUPATIONAL INFORMATION (Use attachment if additional space is needed)

(a) Three-digit Occupational Group Code (From Appendix 2): _____ (b) Job Title (Check Box if Part-Time): _____ ☐

(c) No. of H-1B Nonimmigrants	(d) Rate of Pay	(e) Prevailing Wage Rate and its Source (see instructions)	(f) Period of Employment From To	(g) Location(s) Where H-1B Nonimmigrants Will Work (see instructions)
_____	$ _____	$ _____ ☐SESA ☐Other: _____	____ ____	_____
_____	$ _____	$ _____ ☐SESA ☐Other: _____	____ ____	_____

8. EMPLOYER LABOR CONDITION STATEMENTS (Employers are required to develop and maintain documentation supporting labor condition statements 8(a) and 8(d). Employers are further required to make available for public examination a copy of the labor condition application and necessary supporting documentation within one (1) working day after the date on which the application is filed with DOL. Check **each** box to indicate that the employer will comply with **each** statement.)

☐ (a) H-1B nonimmigrants will be paid at least the actual wage level paid by the employer to all other individuals with similar experience and qualifications for the specific employment in question <u>or</u> the prevailing wage level for the occupation in the area of employment, <u>whichever is higher.</u>

☐ (b) The employment of H-1B nonimmigrants will not adversely affect the working conditions of workers similarly employed in the area of intended employment.

☐ (c) On the date this application is signed and submitted, there is not a strike, lockout or work stoppage in the course of a labor dispute in the occupation in which H-1B nonimmigrants will be employed at the place of employment. If such a strike or lockout occurs after this application is submitted, I will notify ETA within 3 days of the occurrence of such a strike or lockout and the application will not be used in support of petition filings with INS for H-1B nonimmigrants to work in the same occupation at the place of employment until ETA determines the strike or lockout has ceased.

☐ (d) A copy of this application has been, or will be, provided to each H-1B nonimmigrant employed pursuant to this application, and, as of this date, notice of this application has been provided to workers employed in the occupation in which H-1B nonimmigrants will be employed: (check appropriate box)

    ☐ (i) Notice of this filing has been provided to the bargaining representative of workers in the occupations in which H-1B nonimmigrants will be employed; or

    ☐ (ii) There is no such bargaining representative; therefore, a notice of this filing has been posted and was, or will remain, posted for 10 days in at least two conspicuous locations where H-1B nonimmigrants will be employed.

SAMPLE

DECLARATION OF EMPLOYER. Pursuant to 28 U.S.C. 1746, I declare under penalty of perjury that the information provided on this form is true and correct. In addition, I declare that I will comply with the Department of Labor regulations governing this program and, in particular, that I will make this application, supporting documentation, and other records, files and documents available to officials of the Department of Labor, upon such official's request, during any investigation under this application or the Immigration and Nationality Act.

Name and Title of Hiring or Other Designated Official	Signature	Date

Complaints alleging misrepresentation of material facts in the labor condition application and/or failure to comply with the terms of the labor condition application may be filed with any office of the Wage and Hour Division of the United States Department of Labor.

AN APPLICATION CERTIFIED BY DOL MUST BE FILED IN SUPPORT OF AN H-1B VISA PETITION WITH THE INS.

FOR U.S. GOVERNMENT AGENCY USE ONLY: By virtue of my signature below, I acknowledge that this application is hereby certified and will be valid from _____ through _____.

Signature and Title of Authorized DOL Official	ETA Case No.	Date

Subsequent DOL Action: Suspended_____ (date) Invalidated_____ (date) Withdrawn_____ (date)

The Department of Labor is not the guarantor of the accuracy, truthfulness or adequacy of a certified labor condition application.

Public reporting burden for this collection of information is estimated to average 1 1/4 hour per response, including the time for reviewing instructions, searching existing data sources, gathering and maintaining the data needed, and completing and reviewing the collection of information. Send comments regarding this burden estimate or any other aspect of this collection of information, including suggestions for reducing this burden, to the Office of U.S. Employment Service, Department of Labor, Room N-4470 and/or the Office of IRM Policy, DOL, Room N-1301, 200 Constitution Avenue, N.W., Washington, DC 20210. (1205-0310). **DO NOT SEND THE COMPLETED FORM TO EITHER OF THESE OFFICES.**

ETA 9035 (Rev. Dec. 1994)

U. S. IMMIGRATION & NATURALIZATION SERVICE

COLOR PHOTOGRAPH SPECIFICATIONS

IDEAL PHOTOGRAPH

IMAGE MUST FIT INSIDE THIS BOX ►

THE PICTURE AT LEFT IS IDEAL SIZE, COLOR, BACKGROUND, AND POSE. THE IMAGE SHOULD BE 30MM (1 3/16IN) FROM THE HAIR TO JUST BELOW THE CHIN, AND 26MM (1 IN) FROM LEFT CHEEK TO RIGHT EAR. THE IMAGE MUST FIT IN THE BOX AT RIGHT.

THE PHOTOGRAPH

* THE OVERALL SIZE OF THE PICTURE, INCLUDING THE BACKGROUND, MUST BE AT LEAST 40MM (1 9/16 INCHES) IN HEIGHT BY 35MM (1 3/8IN) IN WIDTH.

* PHOTOS MUST BE FREE OF SHADOWS AND CONTAIN NO MARKS, SPLOTCHES, OR DISCOLORATIONS.

* PHOTOS SHOULD BE HIGH QUALITY, WITH GOOD BACK LIGHTING OR WRAP AROUND LIGHTING, AND MUST HAVE A WHITE OR OFF-WHITE BACKGROUND.

* PHOTOS MUST BE A GLOSSY OR MATTE FINISH AND UN-RETOUCHED.

* POLAROID FILM HYBRID #5 IS ACCEPTABLE; HOWEVER SX-70 TYPE FILM OR ANY OTHER INSTANT PROCESSING TYPE FILM IS UNACCEPTABLE. NON-PEEL APART FILMS ARE EASILY RECOGNIZED BECAUSE THE BACK OF THE FILM IS BLACK. ACCEPTABLE INSTANT COLOR FILM HAS A GRAY-TONED BACKING.

THE IMAGE OF THE PERSON

* THE DIMENSIONS OF THE IMAGE SHOULD BE 30MM (1 3/16 INCHES) FROM THE HAIR TO THE NECK JUST BELOW THE CHIN, AND 26MM (1 INCH) FROM THE RIGHT EAR TO THE LEFT CHEEK. IMAGE CANNOT EXCEED 32MM BY 28MM (1 1/4IN X 1 1/16IN).

* IF THE IMAGE AREA ON THE PHOTOGRAPH IS TOO LARGE OR TOO SMALL, THE PHOTO CANNOT BE USED.

* PHOTOGRAPHS MUST SHOW THE ENTIRE FACE OF THE PERSON IN A 3/4 VIEW SHOWING THE RIGHT EAR AND LEFT EYE.

* FACIAL FEATURES **MUST BE IDENTIFIABLE.**

* CONTRAST BETWEEN THE IMAGE AND BACKGROUND IS ESSENTIAL. PHOTOS FOR VERY LIGHT SKINNED PEOPLE SHOULD BE SLIGHTLY UNDER-EXPOSED. PHOTOS FOR VERY DARK SKINNED PEOPLE SHOULD BE SLIGHTLY OVER-EXPOSED.

SAMPLES OF UNACCEPTABLE PHOTOGRAPHS

INCORRECT POSE

IMAGE TOO LARGE

IMAGE TOO SMALL

IMAGE TOO DARK
UNDER-EXPOSED

IMAGE TOO LIGHT

DARK BACKGROUND

OVER-EXPOSED

SHADOWS ON PIC

Immigration & Naturalization Service
Form M-378 (6-92)

APPENDIX A

FILING FEES FOR FREQUENTLY USED IMMIGRATION FORMS

FORM		FEE
I-90	Application by Lawful Permanent Resident for New Alien Registration Receipt Card	$75
I-102	Application by Nonimmigrant Alien for Replacement of Arrival Document	$65
I-129	Petition For a Nonimmigrant Worker	$75
I-129S	Nonimmigrant Petition based on blanket L Petition	$75

(add $80.00 to I-129 if you are applying for change of status and add $50.00 to I-129 if you are applying for extension of stay)

FORM		FEE
I-130	Petition for Alien Relative	$80
I-131	Application for Travel Document	$70
I-140	Immigrant Petition for Alien Worker	$75
I-485	Application to Register Permanent Residence or Adjust Status	$130
I-539	Application to Extend/Change Nonimmigrant Status	$75
I-751	Petition to Remove the Conditions on Residence	$80
I-765	Application for Employment Authorization	$70
N-400	Application for Naturalization	$95

APPENDIX B

IMMIGRATION AND NATURALIZATION SERVICE OFFICE ADDRESSES

ALASKA
New Federal Bldg.
620 East 10th Ave, Rm. 102
Anchorage, Alaska 99501
Tel.# 907 271 4953

ARIZONA
Federal Bldg.
2035 North Central Ave.
Phoenix, Arizona 85004
Tel.# 602 379 3122

Federal Bldg.
300 West Congress , Rm 1-T
Tucson, Arizona 85701
Tel. # 520 670 4624

CALIFORNIA
Federal Bldg.
865 Fulton Mall
Fresno, California 93721
Tel.# 209 487 5091

U.S. Federal Bldg.
300 N. Los Angeles St.
Los Angeles, California 90012
Tel. # 213 526 7647

711 Jay Street
Sacramento, California 95814
Tel.# 916 498 6450

U.S. Federal Bldg.
880 Front Street, Rm. 1-F13
San Diego, California 92188
Tel.# 619 557 5570/-5645

Appraisers Bldg.
630 Sansome St., Rm. 200
San Francisco, California 94111
Tel.# 415 705 4411

Federal Bldg.
280 South First St., Rm. 1150
San Jose, California 95113
Tel. # 408 535 5195

COLORADO
Albrook Center
4730 Paris Street
Denver, Colorado 80239
Tel.# 303 371 3041

CONNECTICUT
Abraham Ribicoff Federal Bldg.
450 Main St., Rm. 410
Hartford, Connecticut 06103-3060
Tel.# 203 240 3171

DISTRICT OF COLUMBIA
(Washington, DC)
4420 North Fairfax Dr., Rm. 210
Arlington, Virginia 22203
Tel.# 202 307 1501

FLORIDA
Post Office Bldg.
400 West Bay St. , Rm. G-18
Jacksonville, Florida 32202
Tel.# 904 232 2625

7880 Biscayne Blvd., Rm 100
Miami, Florida 33138
Tel. # 305 536 5741

4360 North Lake Blvd. , Ste 107
Palm Beach Gardens, Florida 33410
Tel.# 561 691 9446

5509 West Gray St., Rm 207
Tampa, Florida 33609
Tel.# 813 288 1217

GEORGIA
Dr. Martin Luther King, Jr. Federal Bldg.
77 Forsythe Street, SW- First Floor
Atlanta, Georgia 30303
Tel.# 404 331 5158

GUAM	801 Pacific News Bldg. 238 O'Hara Street **Agana**, Guam 96910 Tel.# 671 472 7349	
HAWAII	595 Ala Moana Blvd. PO Box 461 **Honolulu**, Hawaii 96813 Tel.# 808 532 3721	
IDAHO	4620 Overland Rd., Rm. 108 **Boise**, Idaho 83705 Tel.# 208 334 1821	
ILLINOIS	10 West Jackson Blvd., Suite 218 **Chicago**, Illinois 60604 Tel.# 312 353 7334	
INDIANA	Gateway Plaza, Rm. 400 950 North Meridian St. **Indianapolis**, Indiana 46204 Tel.# 317 226 6009	
KENTUCKY	Gene Snyder Federal Bldg. 601 West Broadway, 6th Fl. **Louisville**, Kentucky 40202 Tel.# 502 582 6375	
LOUISIANA	Postal Service Bldg. , Rm. T-8011 701 Loyola Ave. **New Orleans**, Louisiana 70113 Tel.# 504 589 6533	
MAINE	739 Warren Avenue, Rm. 316 **Portland**, Maine 04103 Tel.# 207 780 3352	
MARYLAND	100 S. Charles St., 12th Fl. National Bank Center Tower **Baltimore**, Maryland 21201 Tel.# 410 962 2120	
MASSA- CHUSETTS	John F. Kennedy Federal Office Bldg. Government Center, 5th Floor **Boston**, Massachusetts 02203 Tel.# 617 565 3879	
MICHIGAN	Federal Building 333 Mount Elliot St. **Detroit**, Michigan 48207 Tel.# 313 259 8560	
MINNESOTA	2901 Metro Drive, Suite 100 **Bloomington**, Minnesota 55425 Tel.# 612 854 7754	
MISSOURI	9747 North Conant Ave. **Kansas City**, Missouri 64153 Tel.# 816 891 0603	1222 Spruce Street, First Floor **St. Louis**, Missouri 63103-2815 Tel. # 314 539 2532

MONTANA	Federal Bldg. 2800 Skyway Drive **Helena**, Montana 59601 Tel.# 406 449 5288	
NEBRASKA	3736 South 132nd St. **Omaha**, Nebraska 68144 Tel.# 402 697 9155	
NEVADA	3373 Pepper Lane **Las Vegas**, Nevada 89120 Tel.# 702 4513597	1351 Corporate Boulevard **Reno**, Nevada 89502 Tel.# 702 784 5427
NEW JERSEY	Peter Rodino Federal Bldg. 970 Broad St., Rm 136 **Newark**, New Jersey 07102 Tel.# 201 645 4400	1886 Greentree Road **Cherry Hill**, NJ 08003 Tel.# 609 424 0453
NEW MEXICO	517 Gold Ave. SW, Rm. 1010 **Albuquerque**, New Mexico 87103 Tel.# 505 248 7351	
NEW YORK	James T. Foley Federal Courthouse 445 Broadway, Room 227 **Albany**, New York 12207 Tel.# 518 431 0330 Jacob Javits Federal Building 26 Federal Plaza **New York**, New York 10278 Tel.# 212 206 6500	130 Delaware Ave, 1st Floor **Buffalo**, New York 14202 Tel. # 716 849 6760
NORTH CAROLINA	6 Woodlawn Green, Suite 138 **Charlotte**, North Carolina 28217 Tel.# 704 523 1704	
OHIO	J.W. Peck Federal Bldg. 550 Main St., Rm. 8511 **Cincinnati**, Ohio 45201 Tel.# 513 287 6080	A.J. Celebreeze Federal Office Bldg. 1240 E. 9th St., Rm. 1917 **Cleveland**, Ohio 44199 Tel. # 216 522 4770
OKLAHOMA	4149 Highline Blvd., Suite 300 **Oklahoma City**, Oklahoma 73108 Tel.# 405 942 8670	
OREGON	Federal Office Bldg. 511 NW Broadway **Portland**, Oregon 97209 Tel.# 503 326 3006	
PENNSYLVANIA	1600 Callowhill St., #100 **Philadelphia**, Pennsylvania 19130 Tel.# 215 656 7144	1000 Liberty Ave., Rm 314 **Pittsburgh**, Pennsylvania 15222 Tel.# 412 644 3356
PUERTO RICO	Federal Bldg., Rm. 380 Chardon St. **Hato Rey**, Puerto Rico 00919 Tel.# 787 766 5280	

RHODE ISLAND	The Downing Building 200 Dyer Street **Providence**, Rhode Island 02903 Tel.# 401 454 2865	
SOUTH CAROLINA	Federal Bldg., Room 110 334 Meeting St. **Charleston**, South Carolina 29403 Tel.# 803 727 4350	
TENNESSEE	1341 Sycamore View Road, Suite 100 **Memphis**, Tennessee 38134 Tel.# 901 544 3301	
TEXAS	Federal Bldg. 8101 N. Stemmons Freeway **Dallas**, Texas 75247 Tel.# 214 655 5384	1545 Hawkins Blvd. **El Paso**, Texas 79925 Tel. # 915 540 1776
	2102 Teege Road **Harlingen**, Texas 78550 Tel.# 210 425 7333	509 North Belt (Main Floor) **Houston**, Texas 77060 Tel. # 713 847 7900
	8940 Fourwinds Drive **San Antonio**, Texas 78239 Tel.# 210 967 7065	
U.S. VIRGIN ISLANDS	PO Box 1270 1468 Kingshill **St. Croix**, U.S. V. I. 00851 Tel.# 809 778 6559	Federal Bldg. , POB 610 Charlotte Amalie **St. Thomas**, U.S. VI 00802 Tel. # 809 774 1390
UTAH	5272 S. College Drive, Ste 100 **Salt Lake City**, Utah 84123 Tel.# 801 265 8678	
VERMONT	Federal Bldg. 50 South Main St. **St. Albans**, Vermont 05478 Tel.# 802 527 3292	
VIRGINIA	Norfolk Commerce Park 5280 Henneman Dr. **Norfolk**, Virginia 23513 Tel.# 757 441 3081	
WASHINGTON	815 Airport Way South **Seattle**, Washington 98134 Tel.# 206 553 5956	691 U. S. Federal Courthouse Bldg. West 920 Riverside Ave, Rm 695 **Spokane**, Washington 99201 Tel.# 509 353 2129
WISCONSIN	Federal Bldg., Rm. 186 517 East Wisconsin Ave. **Milwaukee**, Wisconsin 53202 Tel.# 414 297 3565	

NATIONAL INQUIRY TELEPHONE NUMBER FOR THE INS: 1 800 375 5283

FOREIGN OFFICES

Mexico City, **Mexico**
c/o American Embassy
PO Box 3087, Rm. 118
Laredo, TX 78044
(011) (525) 211 0042 x3514

Rome, **Italy**
c/o American Embassy
PSC 59, Box 100
APO AE 09624
(011) (39) (6) 467 4239 x2572

Bangkok, **Thailand**
c/o American Embassy
APO AE 96546
(011) (66) (2) 252 5040 x2614

INS HEADQUARTERS

425 "I" Street, NW
Washington, DC 20536
Tel.# 202 514 4330

There are no INS offices in the following states. Contact the INS office in parentheses for further information.

ALABAMA (Atlanta, Georgia)
ARKANSAS (New Orleans, Louisiana)
DELAWARE (Philadelphia, Pennsylvania)
IOWA (Omaha, Nebraska)
KANSAS (Kansas City, Missouri)
MISSISSIPPI (New Orleans, Louisiana)
NEW HAMPSHIRE (Boston, Massachusetts)
NORTH DAKOTA (St. Paul, Minnesota)
SOUTH DAKOTA (St. Paul, Minnesota)
WEST VIRGINIA (Philadelphia, Pennsylvania)
WYOMING (Denver, Colorado)

There are also four Regional Service Centers in the U.S., which process several of the routine nonimmigrant and immigrant visa petitions. Their addresses are:

✍ Vermont Service Center
75 Lower Welden Street
St. Albans, **Vermont** 05479-0001
Tel. # 802 527 3160

This office has jurisdiction over the following states: CT, DE, DC, ME, MD, MA, NH, NJ, NY, PA, PR, RI, VT, VA, WV and also has jurisdiction over the INS offices in: Puerto Rico, Bermuda, Toronto, Montreal, Virgin Islands and Dominican Republic

✍ Nebraska Service Center
850 "S" Street
Lincoln, **Nebraska** 68501
Tel. # 402 437 5218

This office has jurisdiction over the following states: AK, CO, ID, IL, IN, IA, KS, MI, MN, MO, MT, NE, ND, OH, OR, SD, UT, WA WI, WY and also has jurisdiction over the following INS offices: Manitoba, British Columbia and Calgary

✍ Texas Service Center
7701 North Stemmons Freeway
Dallas, **Texas** 75247-7701
Tel. # 214 767 7769

-PO Box address for petitions, applications,
 responses to requests for information:
 PO Box 152122, Irving, TX 75015-2122
-PO Box address for general correspondence:
 PO Box 36667, Dallas, TX 75235-6667

This office has jurisdiction over the following states: AL, AR, FL, GA, KY, LA, MS, NM, NC, OK, SC TN, TX and also has jurisdiction over the following INS offices: Bahamas, Freeport and Nassau

✍ California Service Center
24000 Avila Road, 2nd Fl, Rm. 2306
Laguna Niguel, **California** 92656

PO Box address: PO Box 30040
Laguna Niguel, CA 92607-0040

This office has jurisdiction over the following states: AZ, CA, HI, NV and Guam

Please note that many states have more than one Immigration Office. If you have a deadline, or need to save time, telephone the INS office to confirm whether the application that you are filing, is being mailed to the appropriate address, or whether it should be sent to a Regional Service Center.

APPENDIX C

U.S. DEPARTMENT OF LABOR OFFICE ADDRESSES

Region I.- Labor certification applications processed for jobs in Connecticut, Maine, Massachusetts, New Hampshire, Rhode Island and Vermont.

U.S. Department of Labor
Employment and Training Administration
1 Congress Street, 10th Floor
Boston, Massachusetts. 02214-2021
Tel.# 617 565 4446

Region II.- Labor certification applications processed for jobs in New York, New Jersey, Puerto Rico and the U.S. Virgin Islands.

U.S. Department of Labor
Employment and Training Administration
201 Varick Street , Room 755
New York, New York 10014
Tel.# 212 337 2185

Region III.- Labor certification applications processed for jobs in Delaware, District of Columbia, Maryland, Pennsylvania, Virginia and West Virginia.

U.S. Department of Labor
Employment and Training Administration
3535 Market Street, PO Box 8796
Philadelphia, Pennsylvania 19101
Tel.# 215 596 6363

Region IV.- Labor certification applications processed for jobs in Alabama, Florida, Georgia, Kentucky, Mississippi, North Carolina, South Carolina, and Tennessee.

U.S. Department of Labor
Employment and Training Administration
Atlanta Federal Center, Suite 6-M-12
Atlanta, Georgia 30303
Tel.# 404 562 2115

Region V.- Labor certification applications processed for jobs in Illinois, Indiana, Michigan, Minnesota, Ohio and Wisconsin.

U.S. Department of Labor
Employment and Training Administration
230 South Dearborn Street, Room 605
Chicago, Illinois 60604
Tel.# 312 353 1550

Region VI.- Labor certification applications processed for jobs in Arkansas, Louisiana, New Mexico, Oklahoma and Texas.

U.S. Department of Labor
Employment and Training Administration
525 Griffin Street, Room 314
Dallas, Texas 75202
Tel.# 214 767 4975

Region VII.- Labor certification applications processed for jobs in Iowa, Kansas, Missouri and Nebraska.

U.S. Department of Labor, ETA
City Center Square, 1100 Main Street, Suite 1050
Kansas City, Missouri 64105
Tel.# 816 426 3796

Region VIII.- Labor certification applications processed for jobs in Colorado, Montana, North Dakota, South Dakota, Utah and Wyoming.

U.S. Department of Labor-Employment and Training Administration
1999 Broadway, Suite 1780
Denver, Colorado 80202-5716
Tel.# 303 391-5742

Region IX.- Labor certification applications processed for jobs in Arizona, California, Guam, Hawaii and Nevada.

U.S. Department of Labor
Employment and Training Administration
71 Stevenson Street, Room 830- PO Box 3767
San Francisco, California 94119
Tel.# 415 744 7618

Region X.- Labor certification applications processed for jobs in Alaska, Idaho, Oregon and Washington.

U.S. Department of Labor
1111 Third Avenue, Suite 900
Seattle, Washington 98101
Tel.# 206 553 5297

APPENDIX D

United States Passport Agencies

Boston
John F. Kennedy Building,
Government Center, Room E123,
Boston, MA 02203
(617) 565-3940

Chicago
Kluczynski Federal Office Building
230 S. Dearborn, Suite 380
Chicago, IL 60604
(312) 353-5426

Honolulu
New Federal Building
300 Ala Moana Blvd.-Room C-06
Honolulu, HI 96850
(808) 546-2130

Houston
One Allen Center
500 Dallas St.
Houston, TX 77002
(713) 229-3607

Los Angeles
Federal Building
11000 Wilshire Blvd.-Room 13100
West Los Angeles, CA 90024
(213) 209-7070

Miami
Federal Office Building
51 SW 1st Ave.-16th Floor
Miami, FL 33130
(305) 536-5395

New Orleans
Postal Service Building
701 Loyola Ave.- Room Y-12005
New Orleans, LA 70113
(504) 589-6728

New York City
630 Fifth Ave.-Room 270
New York, NY 10111
(212) 541-7700

Philadelphia
Federal Office Building
600 Arch St.-Room 4426
Philadelphia, PA 19106
(215) 597-7480

San Francisco
525 Market St., Suite 200
San Francisco, CA 94105
(415) 974-7972

Seattle
Federal Office Building
915 Second Ave.-Room 992
Seattle, WA 98174
(206) 325-3538

Stamford
One Landmark Square
Broad and Atlantic Sts.
Stamford, CT 06901
(203) 325-3538

Washington, DC
1425 K St., NW
Washington, DC 20524
(202) 523-1355

INDEX

Order Form

<u>SHIP TO:</u>

YOUR NAME AND TITLE:_____

NAME OF ORGANIZATION: _____

STREET ADDRESS: _____

CITY:_____STATE:_____ZIP: _____

TELEPHONE: _____

Please send the following:

_____copies of Immigration Made Simple at $19.95 per book

_____copies of Citizenship Made Simple at $15.95 per book

Shipping charges: $4.00 for first book, $1.00 for each additional book.

A check for $_____ is enclosed.

<u>Orders must be prepaid unless using an official purchase order.</u>

Mail to:

Next Decade, Inc.
39 Old Farmstead Road
Chester, NJ 07930
Telephone/Fax: (908) 879-6625